The Collector's
Book of
Railroadiana

The Collector's Book of Railroadiana

by Stanley L. Baker
and Virginia Brainard Kunz

Photographs by Joan Larson Kelly

HAWTHORN BOOKS, INC.
Publishers/New York

THE COLLECTOR'S BOOK OF RAILROADIANA

Library of Congress Catalog Card Number: 75-41800

ISBN: 0-8015-6218-X

1 2 3 4 5 6 7 8 9 10

To my wife,
Myrtle,
who caught
railroad fever from me

Contents

Preface

I can remember the sight of my first passenger train coming down a stretch of track. The huge monster, with bellowing plumes of smoke, breathing heavily and full of scary noises, frightened me. I was out for a walk with my father, who told me not to be afraid and explained how the huge steam engine was taking the people I saw across mountains and plains to faraway cities, even to the shores of great oceans. I was overwhelmed.

As I grew older, my interest in trains also grew. I tried to learn all that I could about them. I would haunt the railroad yards near home, watching engines move cars, switchmen switch track, or an engine being turned around on the turntable. I would go down to the depot to watch the passenger trains come and go. I fell in love with the railroad. I hoped that when I grew up I would be able to work on the railroad, maybe even be an engineer. But my mother thought otherwise. I was frail, and she felt the work would be too hard and dangerous.

My love for the railroad continued. Somehow, I felt I must be part of it. Back in those days, money did not come easily. Sometimes my mother would take me with her to the Salvation Army store where she bought our clothes. One day we passed a counter filled with toys, and I spotted a toy train. My mother said she could not afford it, but from then on that was all I thought about. I would go again and again to look at the toy trains, wishing I had the money to buy one.

Soon I discovered that behind the Salvation Army store was a junk pile where they threw all their broken things, and here I found broken toy trains, which I took home. I would find cars with missing wheels or tops, a broken locomotive, tracks, switches, wheels, parts, and I would carry all of these home to try to fix them as best I could. I made my own railroad layout on the floor, imagining I was the engineer, pulling a passenger train to those faraway places.

One day I learned about the "money dump" behind a roofing manufacturing company. On Saturday mornings the neighborhood boys would dig in the mill tailings for coins screened out from the pulp material in the manufacture of roofing. The tailings were hauled to the dumping grounds on a dump wagon pulled by a team of horses. The driver would pull the lever to open the trapdoors on the bottom of the wagon and dump the tailings. Each boy staked out a claim on the pile and dug around with a stick to see what he could unearth. Coins often would turn up—it was like panning for gold. For the first time in my life, I had a little money to spend and I bought my first perfect and complete toy train.

In grade school, I made another discovery: The railroads were freely handing out advertising materials. I would make the long walk downtown to ticket offices and to depots to collect these blotters, pencils, rulers, pinbacks, memo pads, calendars, timetables, travel brochures, anything they would give me. Soon I had a small collection of what is known today as railroadiana, and I treasured it. I arranged everything neatly in the compartments of two old humpbacked trunks. I would take the items out to look at them again and again, thinking of the adventures they represented. As time went on, my collection grew.

The years passed. When home after serving in World War II, I discovered that all of my collection had disappeared. I never saw any of it again. It saddened me deeply. The task of earning a living pushed my railroad interest aside, but it was always there, in the back of my mind.

Then, like Rip Van Winkle, I suddenly awoke to an awesome reality. The world of the railroads had changed. The steam engine, my boyhood friend, had disappeared from the scene. It was unbelievable. How could this be? I frantically began searching for it, but, alas, the only steam engines I could find were on the scrap line tracks with their fires extinguished forever. I felt as if I had lost my best friend. The Iron Horse had passed on. Never again would I see the steam locomotive in action, smell the puffing smoke, hear the hissing steam and the melodious tones of the whistle, the tolling of the bell, the action of the driving rods, and the clanking sounds the engine made as it went by.

Spurred on by this realization, my search began again for railroadiana. I began to advertise, making the rounds to garage sales, attending antique shows, flea markets, auctions, estate sales. Back I went to the Salvation Army and to the ticket offices and depots, to the railroad yards, picking up items wherever I could find them, building up my collection to what it is today.

I believe that collecting railroadiana illustrates our country's fascinating history to a greater degree than any other type of collecting. The railroads *were* America. My wife and I also collect art, china, glass, porcelain, primitives, Indian relics—all of which are a part of America—but the railroads' history and America's history went hand in hand; they grew up together, attained full stature together, their history intertwined as they both progressed. America at one time had the finest railroad transportation system in the world; the extent to which it has deteriorated today is regretable.

I believe, too, that it is the collector's duty to know his collection, and to know what it represents, what the history is behind it. Just collecting is not enough unless understanding it goes with it. If you are a collector who is content just to possess things but have not made the effort to research your collection, or taken the time to learn about what you have and what it represents, you are missing a great deal.

It is not enough, for instance, to own a collection of railroad wax sealers and simply to display them in a cabinet. With that collection, whatever it consists of, you are holding in trust a collection of historical material. Therefore, what is the history behind these things you have collected? What are some of the stories behind them? When were they used, and how were they used, and why were they used?

Every time you pick up a piece of railroadiana, you hold in your hand a piece of history. For many years this country was in the throes of tearing down and throwing away, making way for something new. This has changed the railroads and it has changed the country itself. But now, somehow, we are beginning to care about preserving these physical reminders of the past. Be thankful, then, for those who, through the years, were the savers—the lantern that was hung in the basement, the shaving mug that was put in the cupboard, the lock and key that were placed in the toolbox, the wax sealer that was not thrown away, the pocket watch that was put away in the dresser drawer, the toy train that was stored in the attic, the postcards and the mementos of the train ride that were put into an album, the calendar that was saved for its picture. Today we are indebted to these savers for those things that we collect. Collectors are the great preservationists of the American way of life and, as collectors, we preserve these things for those who will come after us.

I have not tried to be historically complete in this volume, nor have I tried to picture everything in my collection, or attempted to collect everything it is possible to collect. My hope is that this book, and its photographs, will inspire you to understand the railroad and the part it played in America and to collect its memorabilia.

I have often thought to myself, "What would America have been like if there had been no trains?" Someone once said, "I can no more conceive of a world without railroads and trains to run on them than I can imagine wishing to live in such a world."

Stanley L. Baker

Minneapolis, 1976

The Collector's
Book of
Railroadiana

1 A Wave to the Engineer

History and Folklore of Our Country's Railroads

For many of us, our celebrated romance with the railroad began with long-ago memories of the mournful wail of a steam whistle in the dead of night.

And who among us has not waved at least once in his lifetime to the man at the throttle? Except, of course, those who were born too late to get in on the fun, firsthand, and even they can share in what is truly part of the American experience. Few of us have actually ridden in the engineer's cab, or stoked the fireman's fire, but it is easy to imagine ourselves, as millions of yearning schoolboys once did, at the controls of that enormous engine, leaning out the window to watch the rails shimmering in the heat from the firebox, the wind clutching at striped cap and red bandanna. We remember the orange glow from the open fire door glimpsed across snow-covered fields at twilight of a winter's day.

The excitement of watching the Limited go through was almost unbearable. The thundering locomotive and its churning wheels rocked the station; the roar obliterated all other sound; the rush of air sucked away the breath of the watcher. If this was to be a scheduled stop, excitement would mount before the train entered the yards. The station would be quiet and deserted; then people would begin to arrive, to park alongside the tracks or the depot platform. Taxis would pull up, some with passengers, others to wait for them. How we envied those travelers with their shiny luggage, their air of insouciance. And when the baggage men rolled their carts across the brick platform, someone would sing out, "Train's coming." The whistle for the station stop would be heard down the tracks, and then the huge locomotive would come charging into view.

Today we go to restaurants and bars with such names as The Depot, The Caboose. We use such phrases as "asleep at the switch," "the wrong side of the tracks," "highballing it down the road," "over the hump," "make the grade," "pulling the pin." We use such words as *crummy, deadhead, drag, goat, hotshot, reefer, hotbox.*

Is it any wonder, then, that the great steam locomotives and the trains they pulled are larger than life, and the era they represent part of a past that cannot be recaptured? It is a past, however, that is being preserved by historians, by historic preservationists, by writers, by scholars; and to this august assemblage belong the collectors of railroadiana, who have the best of two worlds: the pursuit of an absorbing, challenging hobby, which is more properly a true avocation, and the preservation of the physical reminders of that remarkable past.

Most of us know the folklore—the story of John Henry, the mighty black driller, of Casey Jones and his classic wreck. We still hear the folk songs extolling their deeds, and we hear *I've Been Working on the Railroad, The Wabash Cannonball, Lonesome Whistle, Orange Blossom Special, The Wreck of the Old '97, Rock Island Line, Nine Hundred Miles, Fireball Mail.* Any collectors of railroadiana should know, if they don't already, that the early sheet music of these and hundreds of other similar folk songs is eagerly sought and highly prized.

We go to art museums and see such masterpieces as Thomas Hart Benton's *Engineer's Dream,* George Inness's *Lackawanna Valley,* Charles Sheeler's *Rolling Power,* Joseph Pickett's *Manchester Valley.*

Collectors will find a *Lackawanna Valley* only in a museum, of course, but they can still find, if they look for them, original oils, watercolors, line drawings, and lithographs of railroad scenes that can be just as satisfying.

We travel about the country and see the majestic palaces that were the great city depots, the delightful little gingerbread castles that were the small-town stations, and the red stone and brick mansions that fell somewhere in between.

Railroads were once magic carpets for a good number of us, and for many they still are. Nothing has quite replaced the sense of a link with far-off, exotic places. Even those of us who grew up in the hamlets of America knew we could go down to the depot whenever we wished and buy a ticket to anywhere in the United States.

And we knew that, if we were fortunate enough, we could ride one of the almost sinfully opulent, luxurious crack trains, such as the Twentieth Century Limited, where vichyssoise was on the dinner menu nightly at a time when it was customarily served only in the finest restaurants.

Someone has said that the invention of the wheel made the invention of the locomotive inevitable. It remained only for man to devise a way to power that wheel, preferably with power supplied by something other than himself.

No wonder camel power, donkey power, horsepower came quickly into use.

The most spectacular advance in locomotion was the development of the Iron Horse. It was the first great achievement of the machine age, and it changed the world forever. Never again would man move at a walk—but, as an interesting paradox of history, he would continue to measure power in "horsepower."

The idea of a steam-powered locomotive did not spring overnight from one man's mind. Almost 100 years elapsed between the first attempt to harness steam and the invention that put that power on the rails. Credit for those long years of development belongs to the British; credit for seizing upon its possibilities belongs to the United States, whose businessmen were the first, after the British, to put steam locomotives on tracks.

The use of tracks for wheeled vehicles was not new. Necessity had mothered this invention as early as the sixteenth century, when roads made of rails began to appear in Europe. These early wagonways or tramways grew out of the simple need to move heavy passenger and freight wagons over rutted roads. Wooden rails were laid over the roads and horse-drawn wagons were hoisted onto these primitive rails. Later, strips of iron were fastened to the tops of the wood rails to cut down on wear and to create a smoother running surface.

By the 1700s the creative genius of the British was at work on the enticing prospect for power that the harnessing of steam seemed to offer. In 1705, Thomas Newcomen invented a crude steam engine, but the renowned James Watt made a better one in 1769 and again in 1774. In 1767, England's Colebrookdale Iron Works turned out the first all-iron rails. They were three feet long and had flanges to keep the wheels on the track. William Murdock built a road locomotive in 1784. In 1804, the great breakthrough came. Richard Trevithick, a Welshman, put together the first steam railway locomotive. It was crude—with its cogged wheels it looked a little like a stripped-down alarm clock—but it was enough to make the world awake with a start to the dawn of a new era.

It is a coincidence that in the same year Americans slowly began to realize how vast their new nation really was, a revelation brought home by the Lewis and Clark exploration of the West. There was land to be settled, but a way had to be found to get there. Destiny and invention came together with a clang. On February 28, 1827, a charter was granted to promoters of the new Baltimore and Ohio Railroad. Within two years, fourteen miles of double track had been laid.

On August 28, 1830, Peter Cooper, a New York ironmaster, accepted a challenge. Cooper had built a locomotive so small that its boiler tubes were made of gun barrels. Appropriately enough, he named it the Tom Thumb. When he was challenged to race his little engine against a horse-drawn car, he accepted. Most of Baltimore turned out to watch. The race was neck and neck until Cooper built a hotter fire, applied more steam, and pulled ahead. Then the belt driving the blower slipped off and the engine came to a stop. Cooper lost the race, but he won a point that was not lost on the rest of the country.

On December 25, 1830, America's first passenger locomotive, The Best Friend of Charleston, pulled out of Charleston, South Carolina. Two wooden wagons hooked to the engine carried passengers seated on wooden benches—the first American-built steam locomotive to haul passengers on a public railroad.

On January 15, 1831, regular service was begun on the line, with The Best Friend pulling the cars. Unfortunately, The Best Friend blew up before the year was out. Steam power was a force people had not yet learned to control; thus, an unsuspecting fireman sat down on The Best Friend's boiler to quiet the hissing safety valve—and the results were explosive.

But Charlestonians were not daunted. By 1833, the line covered a distance of 135 miles. A second steam engine, the West Point, was put on the rails with four cars that carried 117 passengers and traveled a distance of two and three-quarters miles in the incredible time of eleven minutes. The De Witt Clinton, built for the Mohawk and Hudson Railroad, made a trial run in 1831.

Between 1830 and 1850, the railroads were the most important factor in the country's growth. The interest of the public seems to have been immediate. A highly prized and very rare item in the author's collection is a page from a child's primer dated 1835. It has a wood-block illustration of an engine hooked onto one car, and a text that begins, "How fast the cars move. . . ."

By 1835, 1,000 miles of track had been laid and more than 200 different railroads were being built or operated. In 1833, President Andrew Jackson became the first president to ride behind a steam locomotive; he made a twelve-mile journey, but by the time he retired from the presidency in 1837, 1,300 miles of railroads were in operation.

In 1838, President Martin Van Buren signed a bill making every railroad a carrier of the mails, and in 1839 the first Railway Express service was established. The first presidential funeral train carried William Henry Harrison's casket from Washington, D.C., to Columbia, Pennsylvania. Chicago became the country's first "railroad town" with the opening of its first line in 1848. President Abraham Lincoln, who had been an attorney for the Illinois Central Railroad, knew what he was doing when he became a strong advocate of rail service; his successor, Andrew Johnson, made history when, in 1866, he became the first president to use a special train for a speechmaking tour.

At the time of the Civil War, 31,246 miles of track were in operation in the United States, but two-thirds of that trackage lay in the North. This gave the Union enormous ascendancy over the South, which had only 10,000 miles of rail lines.

The railroad did more to change warfare than anything since the invention of gunpowder, and it might well have changed history if the Confederacy had had the rail network possessed by the Union. For the first time, entire armies and their equipment were transported by rail. Victory could be bought with the destruction of the enemy's railroad supply line. Defeat could be assured by capturing a vital railhead, and so the history of the war, as in every war since that time, is replete with the blowing up of tracks and equipment. The classic back-and-forth struggle for Nashville, Tennessee, is just one example of the necessity of controlling a railroad center. The continual destruction of rails and rolling stock was particularly crucial for the South. The region had been more agricultural than industrial and it lacked the manufacturing ability to replace its losses—one reason the Confederacy was not outfought so much as it was outmanufactured.

In 1862, that canny ex-railroad lawyer, Abraham Lincoln, created the United States Military Railway Service, the first organized military rail service in the world, and it has been a part of the United States Army ever since. Locomotives and tenders were painted with the initials USMR, and they had the right-of-way on all Northern lines. Hospital trains also came into use during the Civil War.

When the war ended and the country could pull itself together again, interest in spanning the continent revived with a surge. The need to reach the Pacific quickly had come forcibly to national attention with the discovery of gold in California in 1848 and the launching of what has been labeled the Gold Rush, but may have been the slowest "rush" in history. Although many had talked of railroads west of the Mississippi, not a mile of track had been laid. Instead, gold seekers had to take a clipper ship or steamboat to the Isthmus of Panama, cross fifty miles of jungle by slow caravan, then take a ship up the Pacific Coast to San Francisco. Some opted, instead, for the long way around Cape Horn, while others crossed the plains and mountains by stagecoach or in covered wagons.

In 1853, Secretary of War Jefferson Davis ordered a government survey of proposed railroad routes west and, by the end of 1860, lines had been laid as far west as St. Joseph, Missouri.

On July 4, 1862, Lincoln signed the Pacific Railroad Act, designating two newly chartered railroads, the Central Pacific and the Union Pacific, as builders of a transcontinental railroad from the Mississippi River to the Pacific Coast. The eastern terminus was to be at Omaha, Nebraska, and the western terminus at Sacramento, California.

Ground was broken at Sacramento on January 8, 1863, and construction started on the Central Pacific in May. By 1868, the tracks stretched eastward across the Sierra Nevadas to the Nevada desert. In the meantime, the Union Pacific had pushed its rails west from Omaha and by 1867 had reached Cheyenne, Wyoming.

It was tough going. There was intense rivalry between the two construction crews. They had to contend with the huge herds of buffalo that swarmed back and forth over the tracks, and with bands of Indians who frequently viewed the newcomers with an understandable lack of enthusiasm. The construction crews themselves truly represented an American melting pot, made up as they were of thousands of Chinese laborers, as well as of Irish, Scots, Germans, and Scandinavians, who had played a major role in building the eastern railroads.

The small town of Promontory, Utah, on the northern edge of Great Salt Lake, had been chosen as the meeting point. It was reached May 10, 1869. After six years of great effort, the engines of the two lines moved slowly toward each other until their pilots met. A spike of California gold was driven by Governor Leland Stanford, the Central Pacific's president. Five days later, on May 15, 1869, regular transcontinental service began.

The first northern cross-continental route was completed by the Northern Pacific in 1883. It extended from Lake Superior at Duluth to Washington Territory and the Pacific Coast. The hazards of this era in railroading are graphically illustrated by the Northern Pacific's problems. The line had reached the eastern shore of the Missouri River at Bismarck, North Dakota, by 1873 when the great panic and depression of that year threw the railroad into bankruptcy. It was not until the spring of 1879 that reorganization of the line was completed and work could begin again. Crews and equipment had to be ferried across the river during the summer. In winter, temporary tracks were laid on top of the ice so equipment could cross over.

Among the most fascinating of the collectibles, partly because of the turbulent era they reflect, are the timetables, with such cryptic notations as "Passengers will be conveyed as quickly as possible to the end of the line"— and then apparently will proceed by steamboat, covered wagon caravan, stagecoach, horseback, or any other conveyance that was handy, if not especially dependable.

The Northern Pacific's last spike—not a flashy gold but a utilitarian iron spike, used at the beginning of the line west of Duluth—was driven on

September 8, 1883, at Gold Creek, Montana. The Great Northern did not complete its transcontinental linkup until 1893.

The men behind these major events in American transportation were as individual a lot as the lines they ran. There was the rambunctious Commodore Vanderbilt, head of the New York Central, who said, "The public be damned"; there was the fiercely competitive E. H. Harriman, of the Union Pacific; the urbane Henry Villard of the Northern Pacific; the colorful James J. Hill of the Great Northern. These men tended to have widely ranging interests and to have come to railroading by a variety of routes.

James Hill is a good example. When the St. Paul and Pacific went into bankruptcy in 1873, Hill held the contracts for handling its wood and freight. The line itself was made up of stretches of rails, which seemed to begin and end nowhere. Only two lines, from St. Paul to Sauk Rapids, Minnesota, and from St. Paul to Breckenridge, were completed.

With a number of financial backers, Hill took over the line in 1877. He had spent most of his life up to that time running the Red River Transportation Company, which included hauling freight by wagon or by the squealing Red River oxcarts from St. Paul, head of navigation on the Upper Mississippi, west across the state to the Red River of the North, where it was loaded onto his steamboats, which ran down the Red to Winnipeg, Canada.

A description has been left of Hill's life at this time: "He would spend some time in St. Paul, down on the levee inspecting his warehouse. He would be out on the prairie with his caravans in summer and with his dog teams in winter. His winter trips were made through deep snow, with camping supplies packed on a sled drawn by the dogs. With a guide, he camped out in small groves of trees, melted snow to make tea and ate pemmican. On the Red River, he often could be found in the engine room of a steamboat, repairing a pipe or a leaky valve."

The impact of the railroads on American life was immediate and immeasurable. Between 1870 and 1900, they brought an unparalleled period of growth to the country, leading President Theodore Roosevelt to declare: "Railways are the arteries through which the commercial lifeblood of the nation flows."

There were, for instance, the federal land grants. The first was a grant of 2,595,000 acres to the Illinois Central. Through the years, the railroads picked up millions more acres to sell, and sell them they did. When settlers flocked to take up railroad land, it was easier to sell government land.

Railroads became promoters of settlement. Their agents roamed zealously throughout the eastern United States and in Europe, seeking workers for the lines as well as settlers for the land. Competition was frantic among these men, who were struggling to push the rails farther and farther west, and the need for workers was enormous. The advertising of this need virtually emptied the great eastern cities of their transient population and their arriving immigrants, who came by the thousands, packed on board ship, to ports along the eastern seaboard, then moved west, often under the watchful eye of the agents who had recruited them.

It may be difficult for us to grasp just what the rail lines meant to these men and to their families. Towns quickly sprang up along the lines, towns made up of men who worked the tracks, who cleared land and planted crops, who set up all manner of trade to serve the settlers, who shipped supplies in and shipped produce out.

For thousands of families, the men who ran the railroad controlled their destiny. It is little wonder that, of all the proud men of American business at the turn of the century, the railroad men of the West were the most colorful and the most spectacular and that, as a Briton observed with awe, "When the master of one of the great Western lines travels toward the Pacific in his palace car, his journey is like a royal progress."

2 Everyone Made Money on the Railroad

Antique Toy Trains • Glass Trays • Candy Containers • Shaving Mugs • Occupational Steins • Tobacco Tins • Snuff Bottles • Paperweights • Souvenir Spoons • Cigarette Cards • Calendars • Stevensgraphs • Primers and Dime Novels • Sheet Music • Movie and Circus Posters • Postage Stamps • Greeting Postcards • Pocket Knives • Lantern Slides • Stereo View Cards

Collecting railroadiana is not for the loner who expects to pursue his quarry in some solitude. With well over a million people in the country who are interested in collecting something or other having to do with railroads, today's collector is not exactly lonesome. He finds himself surrounded by his fellow collectors at estate sales, garage sales, moving sales, flea markets, antique shops, antique shows, and friends of friends who have smelled him out. It was not too long ago that he had the field pretty much to himself and could pick and choose.

I had a head start in my collecting of railroadiana, not because of any special prescience, but simply because of an inescapable fact of American life and progress. During the 1950s I realized that steam, as in steam locomotive, was not only going but was almost gone, replaced by exclusive use of diesel fuel.

This, however, was my second time around. I had already suffered that special nightmare of all collectors—finding that my collection had been tossed out. While I was serving in World War II, one of my brothers, who thought I was wasting my time amassing my collection, decided I would have no further use for it and got rid of my entire collection.

So I began all over again, making the circuit of secondhand stores, moving sales, auctions, railroad ticket offices, and railroad men, who would offer me something which I would decline if I already owned one. In those days I was satisfied with just one. If I had bought everything or accepted every item that was offered to me then, I would need a warehouse now. Nevertheless, there is a moral here for beginning collectors. Accept, when offered. In the beginning you usually don't know what you want your collection to become, in the first place, and, in the second place, the problem today is to find the railroadiana collectible, and then to be able to afford it. Any regrets you have will be for what you didn't buy, rather than what you did, and, like every other collector, you will eventually have at least one story about the one that got away.

Enthusiasm for the cause also must be tempered with judgment. With the growing exploitation of the railroad theme, it was inevitable that reproductions would appear. Your safeguard lies in knowing your field, and this means study and research.

There are, in a broad sense, two types of collectors: those who specialize and those who generalize. The specialist may want only those items actually made for and used by the railroads. He even goes so far as to consider those the only "authentic" railroad items. This chapter is not for him or her.

Specialization takes other interesting forms. There was, for instance, the railroad buff from an eastern state who spent the better part of one long hot week during a typical Minnesota summer photographing a steam engine broadside. We encountered him at Cloquet, Minnesota, where steam was still being used on the Duluth and Northeastern Railroad. Each day he stationed himself near the tracks and waited for the train to make its daily run, just so he could take a photograph of it—not a head-on or a three-quarter angle—but a broadside view. He never varied, and he waited all day for his choice shot. He told us that he had thousands upon thousands of broadside photographs of great numbers of steam locomotives, and he traveled all over the country to find them. He had them all catalogued back home, and had journeyed to Minnesota to get these last broadside shots.

Fantastic? Not if you understand the collector's dedication to his quest. We, on the other hand, got up at 2:00 A.M. to make the long drive from Minneapolis to Cloquet to catch the locomotive as it backed out of the roundhouse at 7:00, proceeded to the water tank for the big drink and then to the coal chute for its load of black diamonds. We would spend the entire day hounding the locomotive and its crew during its switching operation in the yards and chasing it on its eleven-mile freight run to Saginaw Junction, where it made connections with the Duluth, Mesabi and Iron Range Railway. We would drive down the highway, stationing ourselves where a long stretch of trackage was visible; there we would wait for the train to bear down upon us, blowing its whistle and belching clouds of smoke; and there we would snap pictures as it went lumbering by. We would jump back into the car and race down the highway to another vantage point to watch again as it rounded a curve, the engine weaving and rocking with its cars. We repeated this process, over and over again, until the galloper headed back for the barn and we headed back for home. Fantastic? Not if you understand the passion of the collector.

Then there was the "depot watcher" who apparently collected experiences, rather than things—either that or he belonged to an entirely new category of spectator sports. This man spent every Saturday night at the Great Northern depot in Minneapolis a few years back, when there were a number of trains still running. He discovered a whole new social caste there, and, as regular Saturday night entertainment, he said, it was better than going to the movies.

The generalist, on the other hand, will collect anything having to do with railroads, up to and including the specialist's "authentic" items. A generalist will be looking for all those items in the form of or in the likeness of the locomotive and its rolling stock, or anything that was even distantly related to the railroads. This is the wide-open approach to collecting. The vast group of collectibles available reflects the extent to which the railroads threaded themselves into American life and the extent to which the glamour and romance of the rails could be exploited by all types of manufacturers of a wide variety of merchandise.

These time-honored "money-makers" are easier to find, simply because they proliferated during the railroads' halcyon years, and so we recommend this approach to the beginning collector. It is surprising how many objects of this type, many of them made years ago, can be found. Some are quite rare, while others are still being made today.

Unless we open our eyes and look around us, we are really not aware of the extent to which railroad-related items have been—and are being—produced by latter-day manufacturers, who are well aware of their potential as money-makers. This general group of collectibles projects the aura of the age of steam, but not necessarily the authenticity.

We might call the collecting of toy trains a generalized specialty, since it seems to offer collectors the better part of two worlds. There are "armchair" collectors and "legman" collectors, and since you can simply buy anything you want if you have money enough, the collectors who "leg" it themselves have more fun. You have the exciting prospect of coming across a rare find in an unlikely place, after you have made the rounds of all the dealers, all the flea markets, all the estate sales, and found it nowhere. And you meet a lot of people. Sometimes the same people. Our search for railroadiana led us to the usual round of estate and garage sales. At all of them we saw the same young man. He had only one question: "Do you have any toy trains?"

Toy trains have had a fascinating history since they were first made more than 100 years ago. Toy manufacturers, even then, realized their possibilities. Even a kitchen utensil firm got into the act, producing early tin-plate trains, which are collector's items today.

It is probable that the first toy trains to be used as playthings were made of both wood and tin; then cast iron came into use. Those of wood were often covered with lithographic paper, which showed the details of the locomotive and coaches, the engineer and fireman in the cab, and the passengers—most often small children—at the car windows. Black-and-white lithographs came first, color later. One of these early wooden trains in my collection has two coaches, both entitled Grand Excursion Train to the Rocky Mountains and California. Beneath the windows, filled with pictures of happy children, it reads: "This is the car in which good little boys and girls may ride." Several American firms made trackless tin pull toy trains as early as the 1840s, and these enjoyed great popularity up until the 1890s.

About 1880 the first cast-iron toy trains appeared, and for the next fifty years these were turned out in great quantities. Both the locomotives and the cars were first made of cast iron, some of them painted in color with a popular red-white-and-blue theme often used. Others were finished in nickel. Later, a combination of cast iron and tin was used, with the locomotive in cast iron and the cars made of tin. Many iron pull trains were still being made during the 1920s and even into the 1930s. These trackless trains are very collectible today.

Friction toy trains were very popular in the early 1900s. These were equipped with a flywheel, mounted on an axle, the ends of which rested on the driving wheels. When a small boy pushed his engine along the floor for a short distance, and then released it, the momentum stored up in the flywheel kept the locomotive running under its own power for a short way. An exciting adventure!

Toy steam locomotives made their appearance in the 1870s. An early American steam engine was made by Eugene Beggs, who patented a model of this type in 1871. From the 1880s on, a wide variety of steam locomotives were imported from Germany, competing with the American-made steamers.

The live steam engine had an alcohol burner with lighted wicks beneath the boiler to heat the water into steam to operate the cylinders back and forth, turning the wheels on the locomotive so that it would run continuously for about a half hour on a circular track. Many mothers feared the live steamers, worrying that they might set the house on fire, causing the manufacturer to advertise them as being "perfectly safe—cannot explode—so simple that a small child can run one safely by following the printed directions." Nevertheless, many mothers surreptitiously disposed of them, not wanting to take any chances.

It only remained for the electric light to replace the gas mantle in homes throughout the country for the electric train to become the most popular toy in the United States. No Christmas, it would seem, was complete for a small boy without an electric train under his Christmas tree. And, as he played with it, he became the engineer, imagining himself rocking along in the right-hand side of the cab as the train highballed it down the track on its way to unknown adventure.

Electricity opened a whole new era in the toy train field as toy manufacturers quickly saw the enormous appeal of the electric toy train to father and son alike. A major hobby today, as a result, it is known as model railroading. Exact replicas of locomotives, rolling stock, and railroad equipment are faithfully reproduced to scale by model manufacturers and by the model railroader himself. This type of railroad enthusiast has a permanent layout in some part of his home, usually the basement, or a temporary setup on the living room floor. It usually includes a realistic representation of a railroad yard, complete with locomotives, rolling stock, and all the equipment, and he can add pieces to his layout by buying them at a hobby shop or building them himself. It is one of today's leading avocations, and Dad is fast crowding junior out of this phase of toy train collecting.

The tin-plate toy train collector, however, does not have it so easy. These old electric toy trains are becoming increasingly hard to find, particularly the earlier models of the popular name manufacturers. Beginning collectors in this field will search a long time before a sizable collection can be assembled.

The Ives Company has been credited with producing the first electric trains. The company, founded in 1868 in Plymouth, Connecticut, was the first major toy train manufacturer in America. Thousands upon thousands of grown-ups today remember the Ives electric toy train from their own childhood days. While Ives dominated the toy train market in the United States, the firm began to experience financial problems and in 1928 went into bankruptcy. It went into receivership to the American Flyer, Lionel, and Hafner Toy Train companies, thus ending Ives's history as a manufacturer of electric toy trains. But the Ives Company has become a legend among toy train collectors. Millions of boys throughout America had played with Ives trains, the beneficiaries of advertising campaigns that urged, "Ask your folks for one for Christmas—a real electric train, patterned after the big ones!" Besides the Ives, there are the Lionel, the American Flyer, Hafner, Dorfan, Bing, Marx, and many other names to look for in your search for an electric toy train. But, as the early Ives ads stated, "Ives Toys Make Happy Boys"—as true now as then for the collector who finds one of these Ives trains in his search.

In addition to electric trains, there are the clockwork or windup trains, which also have an early history. These were similiar to a clock's construction, with a coil spring and a key for winding to self-propel the engine for a short time on a circular track. They were also made by the principal toy train manufacturers, Ives again being the leader, and are very much sought after by the toy train collector.

Your search for a toy train is likely to take you to antique shops, flea markets, hobby shops, secondhand stores, auctions, and estate sales, and no one knows how many attics and basements still hold a yet-undiscovered toy train, intact in its original box, packed away many years ago by some small boy who could not bear to part with it, waiting to be discovered by the collector who will cherish it as its small owner once did.

Because toy trains surface in the most unlikely places, it pays to advertise. Sometimes it can bring surprising results. Some years ago, a family had inherited an estate, which included a toy train they had no use for. At that same time, I had been advertising in the daily paper for toy trains. The result was that I was contacted and was able to buy the toy train, a live steamer complete with cars, made in Germany. This was a happy experience.

Some of these old toy trains are found with the paint flaked off in pieces or with rusted areas, with some small piece broken off, a part missing, or scratched and dented, but this is part of their authenticity. Original old paint, no matter what condition it is in, is always preferable to newly painted pieces. In short, to own an old toy train in its original condition is more desirable than to own a train that has been repaired and repainted. Many an old toy has had its antique value destroyed by a fresh coat of paint that covers up the original lithograph design, lettering, and numbers. Unless it is a very rare item, and is professionally restored by an expert, leave it as it is.

The compelling fascination of the Iron Horse has led great numbers of collectors to search out anything to do with railroads. The scope and variety offered by this general approach to collecting is surprising, even to a seasoned collector.

A great many glass pieces featuring the railroad in some way have been made down through the years, and these form another grouping of railroadiana collectibles. By the 1830s, American glass manufacturers had begun to make flasks decorated with railroad themes. One of these, part of an early series of flasks, shows a horse-drawn cart on a wooden rail, carrying the inscription: Success to the Railroad. These flasks undoubtedly were among the first of thousands of glass pieces that would commemorate the progress of the growing railroads.

Another piece is an interesting glass bread tray with a locomotive as its center design. There was some mystery about this design, and it became the subject of considerable study by collectors, demonstrating the value, not to say the necessity, of careful and accurate research. At first the tray was thought to have been made to commemorate the joining of the first transcontinental line at Promontory, Utah, in 1869. However, research established the fact that the locomotive pictured on the tray was neither of the locomotives that met at the Golden Spike ceremony. Further research uncovered a patent for the tray on file in the United States Patent Office in Washington, D.C., bearing the date of July 4, 1882. This documented data shed new light on the bread tray, and it was concluded that it had probably been made to commemorate the Fast Mail Train, which was first placed in service in 1875 on the Lake Shore and Michigan Southern Railroad, in connection with the New York Central and Hudson River Railroad, on the run between New York and Chicago. The locomotive on the bread tray displays a striking resemblance to the locomotive illustrated on the cover of an 1878 Lake Shore and Michigan Southern timetable in my collection.

Another interesting glass tray is known as the Knights of Labor plate. The design is a finely detailed and generally excellent broadside view of a 4-4-0-type locomotive, typical of those in operation during the 1870s. The baggage car has the large letters USM on it, probably standing for U.S. Mail.

Another eagerly sought glass bread tray is called the Currier and Ives tray because its center design apparently was inspired by the Currier and Ives lithograph, *Some Punkins Beating the Locomotive Lafayette*. The tray depicts a mule-drawn, two-wheeled cart racing to get across the tracks ahead of the onrushing train. The driver is frantically urging the mule to get going and, for this reason, the tray is also known as the Balky Mule tray. Both this and the Knights of Labor tray were made in colors, as well as in clear glass, a popular custom in late nineteenth-century glassmaking.

Then there are all types of glass candy containers, both old and new, in the form of locomotives. The old containers, of course, are the most collectible, and sometimes, if you are very lucky, you even will find one that still contains the original colored candy pellets. Some of these delightful little containers have tin lithographed closures at the rear. These picture the interior of the cab, with the engineer and fireman at the controls. Others have a round tin screw-on cap at the rear of the cab. Its windows show the engineer and fireman, and below are the figures 999, in honor of the record-breaking New York Central engine Number 999, the first train to go 100 miles an hour. Other containers have a tin snap-on closure on the bottom. These candy containers can be found in various sizes. On one, a large four-by-six-inch size, the entire top half of the locomotive forms a detachable cover.

Manufacturers of china were also busily decorating their wares with locomotives. Not surprisingly, many early pieces are scarce, but others still are plentiful.

Perhaps the most popular with collectors of railroadiana, and among the best known, are the occupational shaving mugs. Barbers usually ordered mugs for their customers from the barber supply companies who imported the blank mugs. They were then hand painted with the owner's name and a design showing his occupation, and fired, fusing the design with the glaze. Railroaders' mugs carried various designs—whether a locomotive, caboose, or boxcar, the design showed his occupation. The custom of keeping your personal mug at the barbershop continued until the 1920s, when perhaps the advent of the safety razor made shaving a do-it-yourself project. Most of these mugs were not discarded, however, when the barbershop shelf came down, but were kept as mementos of the good old days, and many were saved by their children. A job with the railroad, after all, was an envied vocation, and none were more proud of his work than the railroad man and his family.

Another collectible is the occupational stein. The regimental stein is one of the Corps of Railway Construction Engineers, and the name of each man is listed on one side. The stein is decorated with hand-painted scenes of trains and bridges. There is a locomotive finial on the top of the hinged pewter cover. The stein is dated 1882-1884. Another stein, a locomotive engineer's occupational stein, is hand decorated and carries the name of the engineer, Karl Gummer, Lokomotiv Fuhrer, across the base. Both steins were made in Germany and have lithopane bottoms.

Other highly collectible china pieces include small Staffordshire boxes in many forms which were made in England during the late 1880s. And, despite their number and variety, in all my years of collecting I have found only two in the form of a locomotive.

A colorful plate was issued in the 1930s by Adams and Company of England. Its center decoration is a reproduction of the famous Currier and Ives print, *The American Express Train*, an 1860s train steaming down the track. This is surrounded by a lush border of roses. A "railway" series of china was made in England some years ago featuring transfer decorations of early locomotives and cars. Copies of this series, also transfer decorated in the same manner, were issued in the 1950s. A reminder to collectors: Be sure you know what you're acquiring—original or reproduction.

Today there are any number of china and pottery items in the form of a locomotive, as the exploitation of the Iron Horse theme continues, demonstrating that profit and proliferation are in direct ratio, one to the other. All of these pieces seem to find a place in someone's collection. There is even a small set with a china engine and cars. Each piece has a hole in the top for a candle and pegs on the bottom, so that they can be stuck into the frosting of some child's birthday cake.

The extent to which advertising has played upon the aura and romance of railroading is fascinating, but scarcely a revelation to the confirmed railroad buff. It has been one of the major advertising themes of all times, ranking along with beautiful women, children, and dogs, but not necessarily in that order. In fact, railroads were acceptable when lovely ladies on cigar boxes were considered rather daring, if not a bit risqué.

Advertising collectibles featuring railroads cover a lot of territory. There is a small tin of Fast Mail Tobacco, with the colorful Fast Mail train puffing across the cover. A bottle of snuff, with its red label, extolls the virtues of Railroad Mills Snuff. A tin advertisement for Pay Car Scrap Chewing Tobacco would urge the viewer to believe that a "chew" was as good as payday, any day.

As a collector, you will pay top price for another fine example of what to look for—the tin advertising sign put out by Altoona Beers. It shows two locomotives winding around the famous Horseshoe Curve outside of Altoona, Pennsylvania. Of all the engineering achievements of the Pennsylvania Railroad, from the bridging of the Susquehanna River to the Gallitzin tunnel, Horseshoe Curve was the most spectacular, and, of course, still is. Approximately four miles west of Altoona, it climbs across the summit of the mountain range and doubles back across the Kitanning Valley to form a great U-turn, the delight of artist and photographer alike.

A great number of metal paperweights were turned out by manufacturers who made products they wished to promote for sale to the railroads. Many of these found their way to the desks of the railroads' purchasing agents, for obvious reasons. While those products themselves would make a fine list of collectibles, paperweights promoting them belong in a general collection. So do metal banks in the form of the locomotive, another "natural" for advertising, if there ever was one. One such bank, advertising the Railroadman's Federal, was no doubt given away to its depositors. Even the cigar industry made use of the train, and it is possible to find these cigar boxes, minus the cigars, with pictures of trains on both their inside and outside covers.

While they are scarce, souvenir spoons still can be found with locomotives, even full-length trains and depots, engraved on them. A good example is the Altoona spoon, with the Horseshoe Curve shown in its bowl and a train on the handle. The spoon is dated 1906. There is also a spoon with an engraving on it of the famous Stourbridge Lion. This locomotive had been shipped here from Stourbridge, England, in 1829, for use on the newly organized Delaware and Hudson Railroad. After a few runs on the line, it proved too heavy for American rails and too rigid to negotiate American curves, and the engine became a stationary source of steam power. The Stourbridge Lion spoon, a souvenir of the first locomotive ever to run upon a railroad in America, is very collectible today, and both the railroadiana collector and the souvenir spoon collector are searching for it.

The bubble gum and football cards had their earlier counterpart in groups of cigarette cards, and for exactly the same reason. The cards featured trains and were printed in England. Many of them were issued by the Imperial Tobacco Company or its branches. The series consisted of fifty cards on such subjects as trains of the world, railway engines, modern railways, railway equipment, and world's locomotives. The front side of each card shows an engine, or a complete train, or a railway scene, while the back carries a description of the picture. Each package of cigarettes contained one card. The objective, of course, was to acquire the complete set, thus selling the cigarettes. The objective of the railroadiana collector today is still to acquire the complete set.

The Travelers Insurance Company seems to have been one of the nation's earliest leaders in the use of railroad themes in advertising. This makes sense, since Travelers had a vested, although entirely valid, interest in the railroads. The first accident policy in America was issued by Travelers in 1864, the oldest writer of this form of coverage. The company usually maintained offices in the early depots, performing the same service the airline insurance machines performed until recently. Travelers' calendars down through the years have carried pictures of locomotives, and these are highly collectible. Besides calendars, I have been able to find other advertising specialities, such as an old pocket mirror, very popular during the early 1900s, with a picture of an oncoming train; a necktie stickpin showing the front end of a locomotive; and a pocketknife featuring a full-length early train on one side, and the name, Travelers Insurance Company, Ticket Department, on the other side.

During the 1860s, Thomas Stevens of Coventry, England, manufactured thousands of woven silk ribbons, which are known today as Stevensgraphs. These pictures were woven on a Jacquard loom, invented in France by J. M. Jacquard, and they had figures in their designs. Thousands of these were sold at the Centennial Exposition in 1876 and, although they had been sold in America before this, after the Exposition they became extremely popular in this country. A very few pictured the train, and these make a delightful addition to any collection. One of them, entitled The Present Time, shows an early engine pulling two primitive cars.

Any railroadiana collector who does not include paper items is missing one of the delights of collecting. As early as 1835, a children's primer, which we were fortunate enough to find, shows a wood block of a very early engine pulling its quaint coach car. The brief text: "How fast the cars move. The car in front is a steam engine on wheels. There is a fire in it, and a large iron boiler, with water. When it gets hot, it turns into steam. It goes twice as fast as a horse can run, and does not get tired."

Children's books issued later in the 1800s and during the early 1900s often had cover designs featuring steam locomotives. That these covers were seldom very accurate as to detail and design matters very little compared with the now-naïve charm of the story between the covers.

Among these were the American dime novel, which captivated so many readers from the 1870s to about 1910, when, alas, the growing sophistication of readers tended to relegate much of this soul-satisfying literature to the attic. There were heroes with names such as Tom Throttle and Dan Driver, who raced to rescue speeding trains from disaster. There was Dick, the Apprentice Boy, in *Bound to be an Engineer.* Dick is shown on a lurid cover as he "quick as a flash, sprung down from the cowcatcher with his rifle on his shoulder," his sudden appearance taking the train robbers by complete surprise.

Horatio Alger's hero usually got his start in his relentless progress on the road to riches by rescuing the bank president's only daughter from the oncoming speeding train. There was no ambiguity with these books; plot lines were simple and direct, and one knew immediately who the hero was. He had no time for soul-searching, he was action-oriented, and he got right on with the business of Success.

These books, by all means, should be collected. They are still unheralded as an art form of the past 100 years, and they make charming reading today.

Diligent searching also should reward the collector with another landmark in the nation's literary past, the Whitman Big Little Books of the 1930s. Many of these told thrilling tales of the railroad, and such books often had locomotives on their covers. Even the *Buffalo Bill Weekly* sometimes featured the train (with Buffalo Bill to the rescue after hair-raising adventures) on its cover.

Popular songs of the early 1900s often used trains as themes for their lyrics, and their sheet music came with colorful covers showing locomotives entering or leaving a station or rolling down the right-of-way.

The brave engineer, in particular, inspired dozens of songs, many of them dedicated to the Brotherhood of Locomotive Engineers. This open admiration of the engineer is understandable. Americans were still adjusting to the idea of speed in travel. No engineer knew exactly what lay ahead of him as he began his run, and the story of him with his "hand upon the throttle," staying with his engine in the face of constant danger, was sung over and over again. It is understandable that most songs hinged on the idea of danger, and particularly of train wrecks.

The most famous railroad ballad of all time, of course, is "Casey Jones, the Brave Engineer," published in 1909. Its cover, with the front end of an engine on it, is a must for any railroadiana collector. Another train wreck in 1903 was celebrated in "The Wreck of the Old '97" (1924) and hinted at in "My Dad's the Engineer" (1895), a song whose sheet-music cover shows a little girl riding the train in complete confidence because her father is the engineer. No wonder Travelers sold safety insurance. No wonder that train wrecks, the most spectacular disaster of that era, were the dominant theme of literature and songs. Other popular railroad songs of that period were "Honeymoon Express" and "Wabash Cannonball."

Collecting of sheet music is growing rapidly today, a reminder of the days when an evening's entertainment centered around the piano in the parlor. The collector should look carefully through stacks of old music wherever he finds them for music pertaining to the railroad. All are collectible, but those published by the railroads themselves are, of course, not only the most desirable, but the most difficult to find.

That great mass entertainment medium of the twentieth century, the movies, always has used trains with abandon. *The Great Train Robbery*, a thundering success, made history as the first American movie to tell a real story with a real plot. Even better, it ended with a bang as the film's baddie fired point-blank into the screen—and audiences all over America screamed and ducked. Since then, the movie industry has found a never-ending source of entertainment in railroads. After all, what better material could there be than the stories of the early trains, as tracks were laid west, as men contended every mile of the way with herds of buffalo and bands of Indians, to say nothing of a colorful assortment of villains hired by rival factions of the Old West.

Collectors should look for the colorful posters that advertised movies with railroad themes. Many of them have scenes from these early movies and they make a fine addition to any collection.

Watch for circus posters, too. That other great mass entertainment vehicle of the past one hundred years depended upon the train so completely that the circus train is as much a part of folklore as the circus it carried. The arrival of the circus train outside of a town in the predawn hours was an event. People today tell of the excitement of watching it pull in. Grown men still talk nostalgically of lying all night in the tall, moist grass alongside the tracks awaiting the train in order to offer their services as water carriers in exchange for free tickets.

The train was the only possible means of transportation for the circus, with its heavy equipment and its animals. How else could it transport the "tallest giraffe in captivity," its huge elephants, its cages of lions and tigers, which had to be loaded on dozens of flatcars? Posters proclaiming these wonders are among the most colorful of this art form, and many featured the train as an inseparable part of the great show. Ringling Bros. and Barnum and Bailey circus often advertised "100 double length steel railroad cars, crammed and jammed with wonders from all corners of the world." Look for these posters; they are being widely collected.

Any discussion of general collectibles should include postage stamps. Here, of course, you will be fighting off the ardent philatelists. However, you will find that comparatively few postage stamps featuring the railroads have been issued by the United States government, a surprising fact, considering the important role railroads played in the settlement and growth of the country. The earliest issue is the three-cent stamp in the 1869 series which pictures a steam locomotive of that era. The second earliest stamp is a two-cent stamp issued for the Pan American Exposition held in Buffalo, New York, in 1901, showing a Fast Express train. The third stamp to be issued was the five-cent parcel post stamp in 1912 which features a mail train.

In later years several more stamps were issued. One is the Transcontinental Railroad issue commemorating the seventy-fifth anniversary of the completion of the Central and Union Pacific's lines. This stamp features a painting of the Golden Spike ceremony by John McQuarrie. In 1950 a stamp was issued to honor the Railroad Engineers of America. This one pictures Casey Jones between two locomotives—one of 1900 and the other of 1950 vintage.

In 1952 a three-cent stamp was issued to commemorate the 125th anniversary of the granting of a charter to the Baltimore and Ohio Railroad by the Maryland legislature. The stamp shows the charter and three stages of railroad transportation. In addition to these, there are any number of foreign stamps commemorating and featuring the locomotive for the collector to seek out.

No railroadiana collectible has more appeal than the enchanting greeting postcards of the early 1900s, which used the train as the theme. Most of them were made in Germany. One valentine pictures a locomotive with red hearts streaming from its smokestack and lovebirds perched on the cab. Another shows birthday greetings being carried by an engine smothered in red roses and blue daisies. Another, an early winter scene, shows a train coming around a curve and bearing New Year's greetings. In the 1960s, the Hallmark Company marketed some lovely valentines with railroad themes. These are collectible, too.

For the collector who is a generalist, the opportunities are limitless. For instance, we found a tin chocolate mold in the form of an early locomotive. And don't overlook the small Cracker Jack train which some child was lucky enough to find at the bottom of the box. If your luck holds, the tiny train will still be in good condition.

Pocketknives were at one time an important part of the various gadgets every man carried in his pocket and these sometimes had trains on them. We found an early pewter matchbox with an engraving of a primitive train on its cover. This is a real collector's item.

Glass lantern slides and stereo view cards, some of them showing train wrecks and many of them showing trains, can be found, too. There are pinback buttons and bookends, and even the lowly utilitarian overall button with an engine on it should not be overlooked.

The variety of items available to the general collector is a graphic example, once again, of the vast extent to which the train was a part of the American scene, and the importance of the railroads and what they represented in the life of the nation is seen in the fact that the value of these collectibles has increased many times since the day they were made.

A passenger coach from an early 1860s wooden pull toy train with glued-on black-and-white lithographed paper reading: "This is the car in which good little boys and girls may ride."

As years went by, colored lithographs were used on the wooden pull toy trains, such as this charming coach of the 1870s showing happy children.

This primitive tin toy train (1870s) was pulled along the floor by a string tied to the front of the engine.

Cast-iron toy engine that a child played with on the floor as early as 1880—a collector's delight today.

This friction locomotive from the early 1900s, when pushed along the floor and released would run a short distance by itself.

This toy train was steam driven and alcohol fired to run on a circle of tracks on the floor. Made in Germany around the turn of the century.

Cars of the live steamer with their roofs opened to show the chalk figures seated inside.

From 1868 to 1928 "Ives Toys Made Happy Boys." This Limited Vestibule Express was one of them.

Locating an old Lionel electric train, which was packed away in its original box, can be an exciting find for the collector.

An old cast-iron trackless cattle train. The engine and cars still have the original colorful factory paint job.

This all-cast-iron pull train is a replica of a Pennsylvania Railroad passenger train from the 1920s, still with its original paint as it came from the factory. The red cars have Washington and Narcissus titled in gold and the black engine is trimmed in gold and red.

Some examples of tin-plate windup trains played with by kids many years ago.

A glass manufacturer made this Success to the Railroad flask in the 1830s showing a horse-drawn cart on a wooden rail.

Two pressed-glass bread trays of the late nineteenth century: The Knights of Labor tray shows a train worked into the border and the other commemorates the first Fast Mail train.

Occupational stein of the Corps of Railway Construction Engineers made in Germany in the 1880s has a pewter locomotive finial and is hand decorated with colorful railway scenes. It has a lithopane bottom.

Colorful plate made in England in the 1930s after a Currier and Ives lithograph, *The American Express Train*.

English china of old and recent manufacture with transfer prints picturing an early locomotive and cars.

Modern shaving mugs with early locomotive decorations, made in England, can still be found today.

Many metal banks were handed out to customers. This one, in the form of an old-time locomotive, is a rail buff's delight.

The railroad pay car, as shown on this old tin advertising sign, is now a thing of the past.

Bottles of Railroad Mills Snuff and tins of Fast Mail Chewing Plug were sold over the counter many years ago.

Not many souvenir spoons have a train on them. This one, dated 1906, from Altoona, Pennsylvania, has a train on the handle and tracks (Horseshoe Curve) on the bowl.

Few Stevensgraphs pictured the train. This one shows an early locomotive and cars and is entitled: *The Present Time—60 Miles an Hour.*

A page from a child's early primer on the railroad.

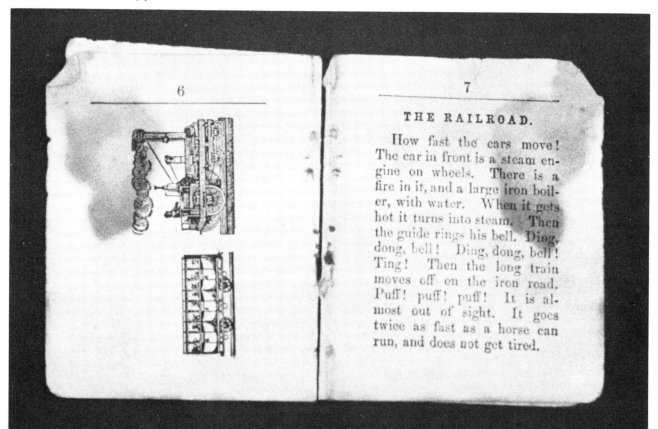

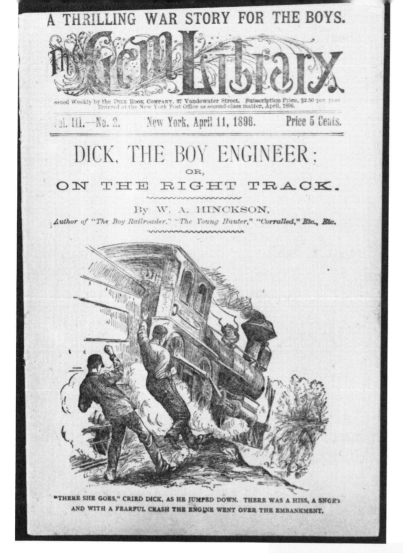

A nickel novel of the 1890s with its thrilling story of *Dick, the Boy Engineer* or *On the Right Track*.

Children's railroad picture books with pages filled with colored railroad scenes and exciting stories were very popular in the early twentieth century.

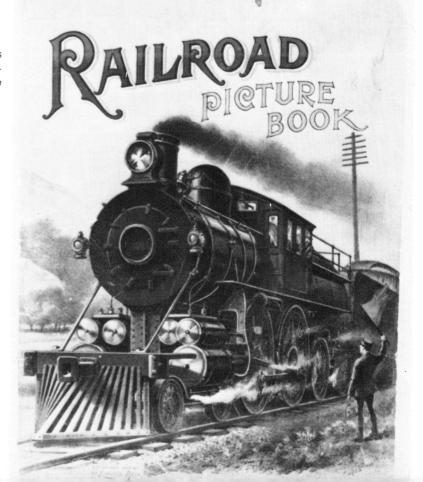

Cigar manufacturers featured trains on the covers of their boxes, and cigarette companies included series cards on the railroads in their packages. Here is a cigar box filled with them.

The Travelers Insurance Company used the train profusely in their advertising from the 1880s on. This rare calendar has a locomotive engraving done by the American Banknote Company.

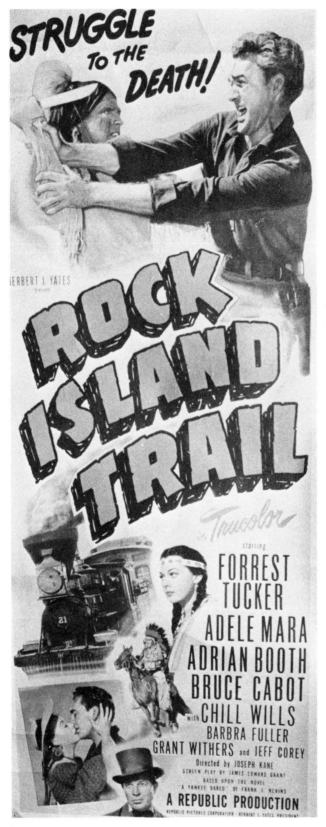

The movie industry made many motion pictures about the railroads, with posters advertising them.

Old stereo cards with trains on them make as interesting viewing today as they did back in the Victorian parlor.

A rare find is this pewter matchbox showing a primitive train.

Even the old pocketknife pictured the locomotive.

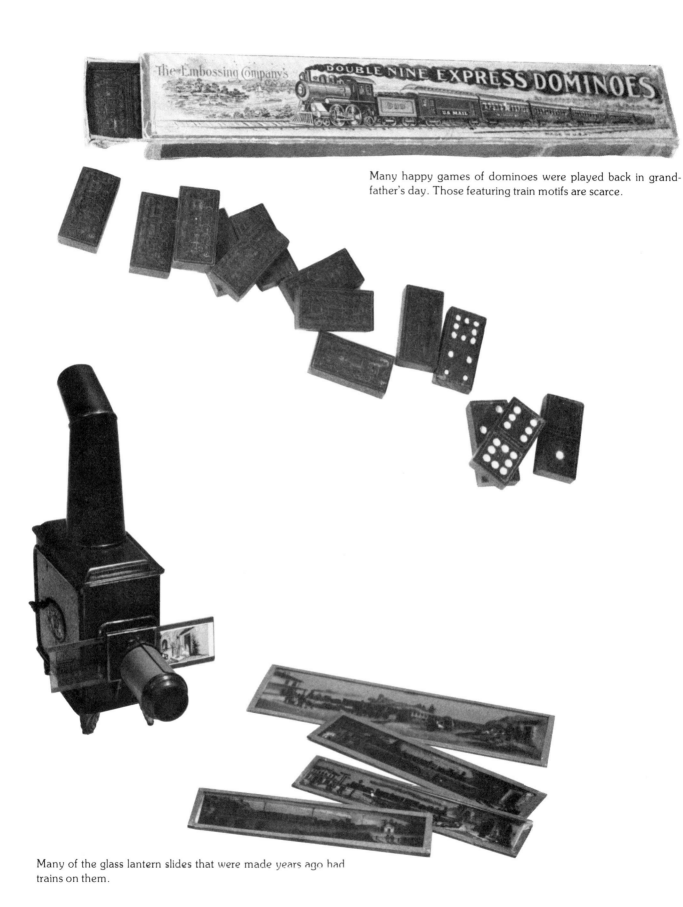

Many happy games of dominoes were played back in grandfather's day. Those featuring train motifs are scarce.

Many of the glass lantern slides that were made years ago had trains on them.

Tin chocolate mold used in the olden days to make chocolate candy locomotives.

China trinket boxes in the form of a locomotive are not easy to find. These go back to the Victorian era.

3 Here Comes the Train!

*Railroad Guides • Textbooks • Cyclopedias • Woodcuts • Drawings •
Engravings • Stock Certificates • Bonds • Currency • Builder's
Locomotive Lithographs and Photographs • Currier & Ives Lithographs •
Handbills • Pamphlets • Brochures • Railroad Calendars •
Photographs • Paintings*

Since the first steam engine moved across the pages of American history, men have endeavored to capture its likeness in woodcuts, drawings, engravings, etchings, lithographs, paintings, and photographs. We are indebted to these artists and printmakers for the pictorial history they have preserved for us of the development of the steam engine on wheels and the impact of that development on the nation.

Locomotive art can be found in newspapers; railway journals; engravings on stocks, bonds, and currency; locomotive builders' photographs; Currier and Ives lithographs; original paintings by famous artists; advertising posters and handbills; the most universal of all art forms, calendars; and in magazines and books. As a collector, whether seasoned, beginning, or just potential, you should not, therefore, overlook the great variety of art that the collecting of railroadiana can bring you.

Early woodcuts of primitive types of trains can be found in back issues of newspapers, railway journals, and other magazines. A remarkable early journal, with the breathless title of *The American Railroad Journal and Advocate of Internal Improvements,* published in 1835, had for its heading a charming woodcut of an early train. The picture shows a locomotive with a pennant labeled Philadelphia flying in the breeze. The middle car resembles a stagecoach and is inscribed Boston, New York, and Philadelphia.

From the 1830s through the 1850s, newspapers carried many likenesses of early trains, as well as listing their time schedules, and early books showed likenesses of locomotives. One such book, published in 1830, traces the development of the railroads from horse-drawn carts on rails to engines propelled by steam. Its title: *A Treatise on Railroads and Internal Communications, Compiled by the Best and Latest Authorities Who Have Original Suggestions and Remarks.* This book, a collector's item, was illustrated with many woodcuts and lithos and with two maps indicating the few miles of existing railroads put in by hand with colored ink.

Waybills and shipping orders of the various railroads often carried cuts of locomotives. Many black-and-white pictorial illustrations of locomotives and railroad scenes can be found in magazines such as *Harper's Weekly,* Frank Leslie's *Illustrated Newspapers,* and Ballou's *Pictorial Drawing Room Companion.*

If you are really into locomotive art, search out those old books and magazines as another fertile and often-passed-over source of railroadiana. They carry a bonus: Their pages contain a wealth of information of great value to the collector, if you would understand your collection. As a matter of fact, it is a good idea to think about building a personal library of railroad books, magazines, journals, published in both the past and the present, as a source of information. You would want to include some of the early *Railroad Guides.* Not only are they well illustrated, but they also contain maps of historical significance to railroadiana collectors and also to the collector of Americana.

The first *Railway Guide* was published in 1847. It had 132 pages, complete with maps. The *Official Railway Guides* and the *Official Railway Manuals* that have been published down through the years contain separate and detailed records on each railroad in the country. The advertisements in their pages are particularly interesting for their information. The guides are also well illustrated with engravings.

Other books include textbooks and cyclopedias on the locomotives and their cars, on engineering, and on railway maintenance. These last were published by the early locomotive companies who were building the locomotives and the cars, and they, too, contain a wealth of photographs and illustrations that are excellent research sources.

Another excellent source of railroad art, and a source that, again, tends to be overlooked, are the stocks, bonds, and currency issued by railroads during their early years. Here you may have to beat off all those collectors whose major interest is in the graphic arts; these old certificates present beautiful examples of a printmaker's art.

As soon as the railroads were granted their charters, they naturally took immediate steps to raise money so they could get on with the building of their lines. And in that free-wheeling and expansionist era, the issuing of stocks and bonds was a natural for raising revenue.

These early stock certificates represent some of the finest locomotive art of all time, first through the use of copperplate, and, later, engravings and lithography. The locomotive theme was woven into their designs. These usually did not show the equipment of a particular railroad for whom the stock was issued but used a standard likeness of a locomotive instead.

Early stock certificates have more primitive designs and weaker colors than those that came later, but they are especially collectible because they date from the earliest years of railroading. By the 1850s the engravings had improved and a finer quality of paper was in use.

There was, however, during those "buyer-beware" years, widespread forgery of all types of stocks and bonds, to such an extent that, on December 23, 1874, the New York Stock Exchange had to issue a ruling that all such documents must be carefully engraved by responsible firms. The result was finely designed engravings with beautifully ornate art in colored inks. The American Banknote Company designed some of the finest certificates known today, excellent in detail.

Collectors may sometimes find a certificate with the signature of an early railroad tycoon. For instance, the name of Jay Gould, at one time president of the Missouri, Kansas and Texas Railway, appears on some of the road's early certificates. This is an added bonus for collectors.

After they were redeemed, railroad stock certificates became the property of the transfer agent, usually a bank. There they were cancelled and filed away in the vault. Some of the agents simply forgot about them. Others eventually destroyed them. Those that survived, however, are as highly prized and collectible as the early prints and lithographs.

One interesting and little-known fact of railroad history concerns the banking privileges allowed the early railroads. Their charters often contained a clause permitting the printing of bank notes, a practice that continued until some time in the 1880s. As a result, railroads printed thousands of dollars of their own money, much of it beautifully engraved with early railroad scenes and locomotives. These also bore a standard locomotive, rather than an engine of the railroad issuing the note. Needless to say, they also are being collected by numismatists, so you can expect a scramble to see who gets there first.

Another form of railroad art is the locomotive builders' photographs and lithographs. Early locomotive builders were dependent upon lithographs for accurate representations of completed engines. These were presented to railroads as the official record of each locomotive. Lithographers such as the American Banknote Company, B. W. Thayer and Company, and Endicott and Company, among others, were commissioned by the locomotive builders to produce these prints. They always showed the locomotive broadside.

I have two builders' lithographs in my collection. One is the *Highland Light*, reputed to have been one of the most handsome engines ever made. It was built by the Taunton, Massachusetts, firm of Wm. Mason. The other lithograph shows an engine made by the Hinckley Locomotive Works, Boston. Builders' lithographs are now collector's items, and they help preserve for us an accurate record of these early steam engines before they were put into service.

With the advent of the camera, photographs instead of lithographs were made by "official photographers" of the railroads. They specialized in taking pictures of the newly constructed engines as they rolled out of the shops. These superb photographs, probably the best ever taken of the steam locomotive, are classified today as "builders' photos" by collectors. They are much sought after, since they are much scarcer than the numerous regular shots taken of locomotives by nonprofessional photographers. All were expertly done, with flawless lighting, no darkening shadows, no background obstructions, and with every detail of the locomotive clearly defined—perfect still pictures of the locomotives before they were commissioned into service.

These photographs date back into the era of the Iron Horse, and again they furnish us with a complete historical record of the engines constructed by the various builders. Some outstanding names of locomotive builders found in these photographs are American, Baldwin, Brooks, and Rogers, to name a few. These beautiful lithographs and photographs are becoming increasingly difficult to acquire, but it is still possible to find them if you search diligently.

On Sundays we used to go downtown and window-shop, looking in the windows of the shops to see if we could find anything having to do with railroads that we might want. If we spied something, we would call first thing Monday morning. That is how we found the Hinckley Locomotive Works lithograph. Since so many of these builders' lithographs and photographs are in private collections, they can be acquired only when a collection goes on sale. That is why regular rounds of antique shops and other types of dealers are important.

Some of the best-known and best-loved examples of all railroad art are the famous Currier and Ives prints that feature railroads and railroad scenes. These lithographs are highly collectible today. Currier and Ives was the best known of the American printmakers, and produced perhaps the most popular of the pictures that have hung on the walls of American homes in the past. They are, if possible, even more popular today, given our current romance with the nostalgia of what we think was a tidy, neat, comprehensible nineteenth-century life. Whatever the reason, these prints, with their scenes of everyday life of the last century, still touch the American people very closely and with immediate appeal. Currier and Ives railroad scenes were a favorite, and today these lithographs rank high with collectors, not only of railroadiana but of Americana as well.

The firm was in business from 1835 to around the turn of the century, and it produced many folio prints in both large and small sizes. A favorite theme was the Iron Horse, in a variety of scenes. Among the most desirable today are those of the American Express trains. However, any original print is a rare find for the collector.

We have in our collection one of the original Currier and Ives lithographs, *The Express Train.* It shows a wood-burning locomotive of the 1850 era with a balloon or funnel type of smokestack. When the best fifty Small Folio Currier and Ives prints were selected many years ago, this print, measuring eight by twelve and one-quarter inches, was the first choice of all ten judges. So, how did we find it? This was a case of collectors knowing other collectors, and who collects what. We knew of a Minneapolis doctor who was one of the first collectors of Currier and Ives originals in this area. When he decided to dispose of some of his prints, as time was running out for him, we learned about it and were able to acquire what we wanted from his collection, among which was *The Express Train.*

Currier and Ives prints are not particularly accurate as to detail, but they make up in charm what they lack perhaps in authenticity. Thus they are completely different from the locomotive builders' lithographs. Currier and Ives artists probably were not all that familiar with how a locomotive worked, or the types of engines in use, but the demand for their prints continues to grow and they continue to vanish from the scene, becoming higher in price and harder to find as time and demand march on.

A note of caution, however: A large number of reproductions have been made from the original Currier and Ives railroad prints down through the years. Examples are the reproductions used by Travelers Insurance Company on their calendars since 1936. Some of these are railroad scenes, including *The Express Train.* Reproductions of many of the Currier and Ives prints are readily available, so it is important to know what you are buying.

Other printmakers have used the railroad theme and there are many colorful historical prints that are better as to detail. The more serious collector of railroadiana may prefer this kind of print instead. Whatever your preference, these old prints graphically illustrate the elegance and grace of the era of the early steam locomotive.

Among the major art works in the country today are the many paintings that drew upon the railroads for their themes. These early railroad paintings reflect the era in which they were painted, a time of railroading never to be forgotten, and thus they tell the story of the growth of America.

There is the famous *Lackawanna Valley* by George Inness, who was a struggling young artist when he painted it in 1854 for George D. Phelps, first president of the Delaware, Lackawanna and Western Railroad. It shows the road's early roundhouse at Scranton, Pennsylvania, and one of the three engines owned at the time. There is even a figure off to one side watching— an early train-watcher, perhaps, or railfan. The painting was lost for many years, but in 1892 Inness himself found it in Mexico and brought it back to this country. It now is in the National Gallery of Art in Washington, D.C.

The *9:45 A.M. Accommodation, Stratford, Conn.*, painted in 1867 by Edward Lamson Henry, hangs in New York's Metropolitan Museum of Art. This is a painting which graphically shows us the extent to which, even then, a town's activity centered around the railroad depot, the lifeblood of the community where, as the train came and went, the town's business was transacted.

Then there was Thomas Hart Benton's *Wreck of the Old '97*, in which the locomotive hits a broken rail "going down the grade at ninety miles an hour," as the song says. Benton added a horse and wagon to the scene, with the horse bolting and upsetting the occupants. He explained later, "It doesn't say who saw it happen, but somebody must have, and it could just as well have been people like those in the wagon. I put 'em in anyway."

Of course, the originals of other classics also are now, for the most part, in museums, where they are every bit as enjoyable. You can buy beautifully reproduced prints in a variety of sizes for a surprisingly small amount of money.

However, you can still find original works by artists who painted railroad scenes, whether they worked in oils, watercolors, lithographs, or line drawings. They may not be as well known, but those of us who are railroadiana collectors appreciate their work just as much.

As the twentieth century got under way, the railroads, with their luxury equipment, dominated the American scene. Many artists captured the beauty of the passenger train at a time when railroading was at its best. The late Helmut Kroening, a St. Paul artist, is a good example of the artist of this period. He had loved the steam engine since early boyhood and this feeling has given his paintings an accuracy of detail and realism that is thrilling for a confirmed railroad buff to see.

During the 1920s and 1930s, the railroads sought out artists to paint their crack Limited trains. These paintings were for framing for the companies' offices and for use on their calendars. The paintings of Grif Teller, Walter L. Greene, and William Harnden Foster, for instance, were reproduced on calendars for the Pennsylvania Railroad and the New York Central. Through the years the calendars have made the work of these men familiar to every railroadiana collector.

Another railroad artist of this period, A. Sheldon Pennoyer, began to paint railroad scenes in 1928. He drew upon periods in American transportation history for his themes. He used early illustrations, photographs, and Currier and Ives lithographs for his subjects, but he infused his work with his own lifelong love for the steam engine. His paintings, now in the collections of many of the large railroads, as well as in museums and private collections, are highly prized today.

There also are many contemporary artists who are now, for the first time in a long, long time, beginning to portray the steam locomotive, partly because of the revived interest in the old steam locomotives and the galloping nostalgia concerning the railroads in general. This has created a ready market for railroad pictures, a fact of life which today's artists understand thoroughly, as did their peers of the past. The work of today's artists, who are painting in retrospect, undoubtedly will become the collectibles of the future.

Howard Fogg's paintings are perhaps the most familiar to railroadiana collectors today. Many of them have been reproduced in color in the famous Beebe and Clegg railroad books. Other examples of railroad art that have appeared on magazine covers and in railroad books are the works of Otto Kuhler, William Wakefield, Herb Mott, Gil Reid, Frederick Blakeslee, and W. C. Merritt, to name a few. These men have lived and painted during the years of steam. Many of their paintings are in private collections, and they will continue to be in demand.

Then there is the kind of art that you can participate in yourself, the creation of your own paintings. When I stopped working some years ago, upon the advice of my doctor, I began to paint my own oils of railroad scenes. I was particularly interested in western themes, partly because I had noticed something about the western paintings that was fascinating by its omission. The great western painters, such as Remington and Russell, had simply wiped the steam engine from the scene, as far as their paintings were concerned. Yet, during their era, the steam engine was very much a part of western life. Cowboys drove their herds to the railhead; Indians, as well as mountain men, fought off the railroads; cattlemen shipped their beef by train; farmers shipped produce out, supplies in, by rail; the vast herds of buffalo continually stopped the trains; and a locomotive blowing its whistle would often spook horses and cattle into a stampede.

Yet, very little of this is reflected in the works of Russell and Remington, to name the two major artists of this period. Apparently both men resented, even hated, the railroads because they knew they would change the West. Remington disliked the coming of the Iron Horse just as Russell cursed the introduction of barbed wire to the open range. They realized that the West they knew and loved would disappear, gone forever in the name of progress.

And so I began to paint western scenes which would reflect the tremendous role the railroads played in the settlement of the West. I also paint contemporary scenes, such as a little old depot sitting on a station platform, overgrown with weeds. If you feel you cannot paint—and I urge you to try it, at least—then use your camera. Look for scenes you really would like to capture on film. They are all around you. Remember that today photography has become an art form, too, and railroad magazines are full of advertisements for photographs.

As the iron rails spread across the continent, the advertising on the part of the railroads for passengers spread over the country, too, and produced some of the liveliest of American art. Whether it was to lure the traveler or the settler, nothing since has surpassed the railroad advertising brochure in imagination and exuberance.

At first, art work consisted chiefly of lithographs, and these have preserved for all time the likenesses of those early locomotives. Posters, leaflets, broadsides, and handbills all carried lithographs of engines and cars. These were produced in great numbers, and they are invaluable to the collector today because they portray railroading as it was in its earliest years.

In 1834, the Mohawk and Hudson Railroad issued a poster advertising a "Packet Boat and Rail-road Arrangement," showing a packet boat meeting the train. The poster advised its readers that a "packet boat will leave Schenectady daily, for Utica, Rochester and Buffalo, at half past 10 o'clock A.M. and half past 6 o'clock P.M. Passengers for the packets will leave Albany by the cars at 9 A.M. and 5 P.M. These are the only cars that run to the packets. By this Arrangement, there is no delay, as the packets will leave Schenectady immediately after the arrival of the cars." The Pioneer Fast Line's railroad poster for 1837, also with an early train illustrated, announced that passengers could travel from Philadelphia to Pittsburgh in three and a half days via railroad, portage, and canal, then catch a steamboat down the Ohio river to Louisville, Kentucky.

Most of these early advertising lithographs were black-and-white, and they proliferated as the railroads competed in their struggle for business.

By the latter half of the nineteenth century, a new element was introduced. The federal government ushered in the land grant era, which has had mixed reviews ever since. Nothing was the matter with the theory: The government would make grants to the railroads of land on either side of their tracks; ergo, the presence of the railroads would attract settlers to these lands as well as to the millions of acres still owned by the government. Up to this time the government lands had gone begging.

The theory worked. The railroads quickly became the greatest real estate salesmen in history. With millions of acres to sell, they attracted settlers through a flood of posters and pamphlets, enthusiastically proclaiming these "acres of wonderland." The early advertising handbills were issued to lure both immigrants and unhappy eastern farmers to new farms, and they are filled with grand allusions to the "promised lands" awaiting them. From 1850 to 1871 alone, the government gave the railroads 130,000,000 acres of land.

The first railroad to receive a sizable grant was the Illinois Central, with 2,595,000 acres. The railroad promptly advertised:

> Best Farming Lands in the World. For sale by the Illinois Central Railroad in tracts to suit purchasers at low price, for those whose limited means forbid the purchase of a homestead in the older states. 900,000 acres of the best farming land in the country, soil of unsurpassed fertility; the climate is healthy, taxes are low, churches and schools are becoming abundant through the length and breadth of the state, and communication with all the great markets is made easy through railroads, canals and rivers. Grain and stock-raising, cotton, flax, fruit, corn, land, lumber.

Practically every newspaper in the United States had an Illinois Central ad. In Germany, Scotland, Sweden, Norway, Ireland, England, agents of the Illinois Central peddled its handbills, pamphlets, and posters, many picturing bumper crops of wheat and corn, with well-fed cattle grazing off the fat of the land. And the people believed it. Thousands started westward, believing that "California gold, in years to come, cannot hope to match the unlimited resources of Illinois. In iron, lead, zinc and limestone, we are unlimited; and as yet these matchless resources, the eventual fountainhead of great wealth, have scarcely been touched."

Naturally, other railroads also turned to these advertising handbills, posters, and pamphlets, which were often more interesting than accurate. While this colorful propaganda was aimed at eastern farmers, they also were translated into more than ten languages to reach hopeful, land-hungry peasants in Europe. It was buyer-beware all over again. Western plains were described as a well-watered garden, bearing no resemblance to the "Great American desert" it has been called. Yields of 50 bushels of wheat per acre and 100 bushels of corn are glowingly described. Kansas's long, brutal winter is described as being only two months long, with coal plentiful if wood gave out. Minnesota's climate is pictured as downright salubrious, known to heal every ill of mankind.

The Northern Pacific advertised that "the Best Homes for 10,000,000 people now await occupancy in Minnesota, North Dakota, Montana, Northern Idaho, Washington and Oregon!" The handbill went on:

2,000,000 families—10,000,000 Souls! Of the Great Population—no man can predict how great it will become—which will soon inhabit this vast region, the new comers from the older states will become the first families, and leaders, socially and politically, in this newly opened section of the United States. They will all become prosperous, and many will acquire fortunes in a short period, by turning the vast wheat-producing lands, ready for the plow, into productive farms; by stockraising, on the immense grazing ranges; by developing the resources of the extensive forests and mineral districts; by engaging in various trades and manufacturing enterprises; and by investments in the thriving new towns and other property in the vast region opened for settlement all along the line of the *Northern Pacific Railroad.*

Beginning in the 1880s, immigration into Northern Pacific lands flourished. In 1880 the Great Northern sold a million dollars worth of land along its route. Jim Hill sent his agents to the Scandinavian countries, as he believed these hardy people ideally suited for the climate of the lands through which his road traveled, promoting the "Northwestern States." His pamphlet, *Minnesota As It Is*, advised readers that "if you are not a good farmer, go to Kansas or New Mexico, where the winds and sands will help the people make it hot for you." Hill often took the time to visit the new settlements his advertising had established. Many of the railroads spent huge amounts of money on wooing settlers. Some roads provided board and room for those who wanted to shop around for a farm site; other roads sold lands for little more than two dollars an acre. The Rock Island advertised that the emigrants would be carried on their Express trains from Chicago to the Missouri River on good coaches, nicely cushioned, well warmed in winter and well ventilated in summer. The line further stated that "West of the Missouri River the Pacific Railroads are now running their *New Style Third Class* sleeping cars attached to third class trains, giving each passenger therein a bunk or berth. These cars have raised roofs, Miller platforms and couplings, air brakes, and are divided off similarly to first-class cars, having 12 sections capable of seating or berthing 4 persons to a section, making a total capacity of 48 persons to the car. These cars afford comfortable sleeping accommodations for such passengers. The seats by the sliding process forming the lower berths, and to each section a double partitional upper berth is arranged lineal from the side of the car. The passengers providing themselves with a cheap mattress and necessary blankets; besides the berths, these cars are fitted with large water tanks, connecting wash basins, stoves at each end. No extra charge is made for berths. The time from the Missouri River to San Francisco by emigrant train is about nine days." They further stated that "the difference in time between the Missouri River and San Francisco between first-class and emigrant train is about four days"—which meant that half the time the emigrant sat in the train as it waited on the siding for first-class trains to go by them.

The results were without precedent. The 30 years between 1870 and 1900 were the years of overwhelming response to the call of wide-open acreage; more land was settled during those years than during the 250 years since the founding of Plymouth Colony. Settlers poured into the midwest, Minnesota, the Dakotas, Montana, the South, the Southwest, California, and the Pacific Northwest.

Of course, the reality of drought, blizzards, grasshoppers, and fires soon set in, and many moved back east, but immediate replacements appeared and eventually stayed.

This national phenomenon led Congressman Charles E. Hooker to declare that the nation gave the railroads "an empire composed of an arid desert unfit for the habitation of man," and the railroads, as a result of their intensive promotion, returned to the country "an empire of hardy and industrious citizens." It is little wonder that these advertising posters and handbills and brochures, with their extravagent phrases and impossible promises, are of great interest to the collector of railroadiana.

There was, however, a serious problem for the unsuspecting emigrant, once he was no longer under the watchful eye of the railroads' agent. In 1850 the following notice to emigrants was published by the Sacramento Settlers Association to warn them against crooked agents selling free lands.

> *Notice to Immigrants*
> As there are in our city a number of men with remarkable principles who go among those who have newly arrived and offer to sell or lease to them the public land in and about this place, thus imposing upon the unsuspecting, the latter are hereby notified that the vacant land in Sacramento City and vicinity are all free of charge, but they can make either of the following gentlemen a present of a few thousand dollars if they have it to spare. Such favors are eagerly sought and exstringently received by them. In fact, some of them are so solicitous in this matter that if they are not given something they will almost not like it and even threaten to sue people who will not contribute to their support. They who have made themselves the most notorious are [and the notice lists twenty-five names].

Antirailroad propaganda often turns up, too, as in this soul-searing broadside: "Mothers, Look Out for Your Children! Panicked Cities! Dreadful Casualty! When you leave your family in health, you must be hurried home to mourn a dreadful casualty. Locomotive Railroad through your beautiful streets is the ruin of your trade, annihilation of your rights, and regardless of your property and comfort. Will you permit this? Rally people in the majesty of your strength and forbid this outrage." Worried canal and coastal shipping stockholders often sponsored this type of scare appeal.

The services railroads provided stretched into other areas as well, as, in 1884, the New York Central and Hudson River Railroad advertised the following:

> *Important to Residents of Brooklyn:* The completion of the New York and Brooklyn Bridge, and the successful running of the cars on the Bridge Railway, opens up (in connection with the Third Avenue Elevated Road) a quick and reliable route between the Grand Central Depot and Brooklyn, reducing the time to about 30 minutes.

And, to:

> *Tourists and Others* arriving in New York by Atlantic steamers will be met at the Barge Office by a representative of this company, whose duty it is to obtain tickets, seeing to checking of baggage, etc., etc., and to carefully look after the comfort and convenience of passengers traveling via this line.

The colorful travel posters put out by the railroads are especially interesting. On May 10, 1869, as soon as transcontinental travel became a reality, the Union Pacific issued its famous art poster advertising the grand opening of rail travel from the Atlantic to the Pacific. No doubt it was the first of the art advertising posters that lured tourists with their promises of restful, elegant palace sleeping cars, comfortable reclining-seat parlor cars, and unsurpassed meals in dining cars.

The Chicago and Northwestern Railway in 1879 advertised that

> no other road runs Pullman hotel cars, Pullman dining cars, or any form of dining, hotel, or restaurant cars through between Chicago and Council Bluffs.
>
> The Palatial Hotel Cars, "West Bend," "International," and "St. Nicholas," were constructed especially for the "Pioneer Line," and are the finest cars ever built by the Pullman Palace Car Co. These "Modern Hotels," please note, are not dining cars which are run only a few miles and then switched off, but are truly what their names imply, "Palatial Hotel Cars," each containing a neat, cozy and clean kitchen, with china, glass and cutlery closets; a *Grand Saloon* consisting of 12 sections, with space in each for a table where meals are served. An elegant *Drawing Room* in which the occupants can be entirely secluded from the grand saloon if desired, conveniently arranged *Lavatories* and *Compartments* for separate use of ladies and gentlemen; supplied with every needed article to perfect an elaborate toilet. A passage way and air chamber separates the saloon from the kitchen, which effectually prevents any odors from the cooking viands from reaching the occupants of the car.
>
> In the *Hotel Cars* meals are served a la carte—hence you pay for what you get and nothing more, and good meals can be got for 50 to 75 cents.
>
> At night the grand saloon and drawing room are changed into a boudoir where your bed is prepared and you rest for the night as in a private bedroom.
>
> It is no exaggeration to say the world does not produce the equal of these magnificent cars.

The Baltimore and Ohio advertised in 1886 that it had

> never been in the habit of consulting the desires or happiness of competing companies, having sufficient to absorb all of its time in looking out for the comfort and convenience of its patrons.

They further stated that

> Nothing it has given them has proved more satisfactory than the limited trains upon which not a nickel of extra expense is charged, and upon which a man goes as he pleases, paying for what he may wish, and realizing that he is in a country free as to railroad choice as in anything else. The record of the B & O limited trains is something to be proud of, and the reputation they have made for being on time has never been surpassed in the world. The trains of the B & O are models of latter day elegance and comfort. Not only is the ease of the outer man so carefully looked to, but of the inner man as well, the dining cars and dining halls being simply beyond comparison.

As the years passed, the famous name trains of the 1900s were featured on railroad advertising prints, all of which are highly collectible today. With more modern, sophisticated methods, railroad advertising eventually changed greatly, and the early advertising material slowly disappeared. However, much still was saved, and it can still be found today by collectors who search diligently.

The travel brochures of the 1920s and 1930s continued to lure the traveler. These were the peak years of train travel in America, and they lasted until World War II. Tours of all kinds were offered, such as the 1933-1934 Chicago Century of Progress Exposition tours. As a Milwaukee Road travel brochure pointed out, American history and railroad history coincided in the same 100 years, both illustrating America's 100 years of progress. New equipment, the dome cars, the change from steam to diesel, all were highlighted in railroad advertising brochures. These are invaluable today, not only to collectors of railroadiana but to collectors of Americana, and to general historians, also. The brochures contain rare photographs of places of interest, of old depots and buildings, of railroad equipment, of new inventions, of interesting early maps, and much, much else that has since vanished from the American scene. Many brochures picture early train interiors, fashions of the period, interiors and facades of buildings long since torn down. Many of these pictures can be found nowhere else. A part of America's past is contained in them.

Not many railroad calendars of the 1880s and 1890s have survived. When they can be found at all, many are in less than perfect condition, with their monthly pages missing. But their Victorian appearance, with pictures of steam locomotives and cars and of railroad scenes of that earlier era, makes them highly collectible, and the collector who finds one is fortunate, especially if it is in excellent condition. He's lucky, as a matter of fact, if it's in merely good condition, which means that at least some of the monthly pages are still intact.

The railroads were great believers in this form of advertising. They handed out their calendars freely each year, and hung them conspicuously on the walls of their ticket offices and depots. Many railroad paintings were reproduced for calendar use. When the year had passed, and the monthly pages no longer were intact, their pictures were saved and framed, and these still can be found well preserved behind the glass, in their original frames.

An example: We came upon a dilapidated old school bus at an open air flea market one Sunday afternoon when we were making the usual rounds in our search for railroadiana. The dealer had made the bus into a mobile antique shop, and he made the rounds of the flea markets, hanging out his shingle, inviting all to come inside and browse. We accepted the invitation.

There was a narrow aisle down the center of the bus, with "junque" on either side and to the rear wall. Finding nothing, we started to leave, and turned our attention to the dealer who was sitting at a makeshift table close to the steering wheel, eating a bologna sandwich and washing it down with a bottle of soda pop.

Suddenly, partially obstructed from view behind him, I caught sight of a picture hanging on the wall, and held my breath. There was a framed New York Central calendar print of the Twentieth Century Limited, painted by William Harnden Foster in 1922! When I asked the inevitable question, "Is that picture for sale?" he jokingly remarked, "Everything is for sale, including the bus." I shared his humor. I told him that I collected railroad artifacts, and asked again if the picture was for sale. He said it was, and I bought it—so typical of a place where you would least expect to find a picture of this kind.

New York Central's famous art calendars of the 1920s featured their speeding name passenger trains. Now, a half century later, you still may come across them. To find one that has never been used, with the flyleaf intact, is a collector's dream. Through an ad in one of the antique publications, I found a 1926 calendar of the New York Central in mint condition, never used—another lucky find. It carries a picture of the Twentieth Century Limited, the line's standard-bearer. Titled *A National Institution*, it was painted by Walter L. Greene.

The Pennsylvania Railroad also used its famous name trains on its calendars during the years when steam was king. These were painted by Grif Teller, and are in great demand today, too.

In 1928, the Great Northern Railway began publication of a series of monthly calendars featuring reproductions of Winhold Reiss's portraits of the Blackfoot Indians of Glacier National Park. These portraits have become universally known today because of these attractive and colorful calendars, with their immense circulation.

Other railroads have published calendars featuring both steam locomotives of the past and diesels of the present. A collection of these represents a fascinating segment of railroad history down through the years. Many calendars are from railroads no longer in existence, and the remaining roads are putting out fewer and fewer calendars. Don't overlook these, either, since, once again, they are the collectibles of the future.

Early photographs of railroad scenes and locomotives make up still another grouping of collectibles. They are of immense interest both to collectors and to general historians because, again, they document the history of railroading in America. As a result, there has been a steadily growing appreciation of them. Photographs today are a widely recognized art form. The old railroad photographs from no longer existing glass negatives are undoubtedly rare.

Many of the railroads had official photographers who recorded the road's progress down through the years on glass plate or film. For instance, official photographs by F. Jay Haynes, the Northern Pacific's official photographer, traced the fortunes of that railroad beginning with the track hands that laid down the rails to the West. The result of Haynes's work is a complete record of the immense difficulties the N. P. encountered on its way to the Pacific.

The Pennsylvania Railroad had a fine photographic record made of all its locomotives from the 1850s through the 1870s. W. T. Purviance photographed a series of scenes along the Pennsy's route. Many of these became stereo cards for use with the stereoscopic viewers that were a fixture of Victorian parlors. Most old photographs are in black and white, although some have a monochrome finish; fewer are colored.

By the early 1900s, the railroads had begun to use more and more photographs to publicize their passenger trains and their scenic routes. Again, many of these publicity photos are in black and white, but some are in color—a growing number, as time went on. They often were framed for display in ticket offices, depots, and business offices. All of these old photographs are very collectible today.

In later years, as the camera came more and more into use by the general public, the photographing of locomotives and railroad scenes grew to such proportions that today it has become a large-scale hobby among railroad enthusiasts. (Remember the man at Cloquet.) Many thousands of pictures have been taken of both steam and diesel locomotives. Collectors of railroad pictures can fill albums with candid railroad shots available through advertisements in hobby and collectors' magazines.

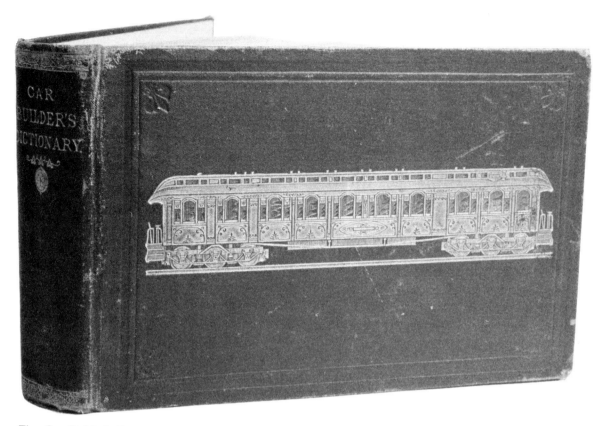

The Car Builder's Dictionary, published in 1881, is a well illustrated book covering the early rolling stock of American railroads during that period.

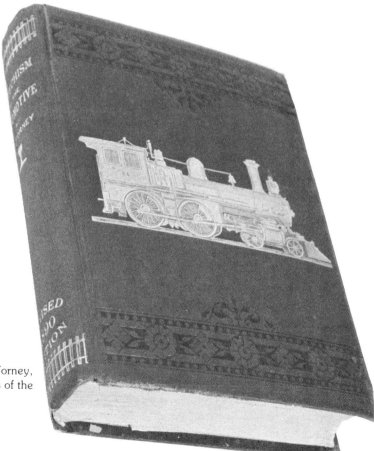

Catechism of the Locomotive by Matthias N. Forney, published in 1890, concentrates on the physical aspects of the steam locomotive of the times.

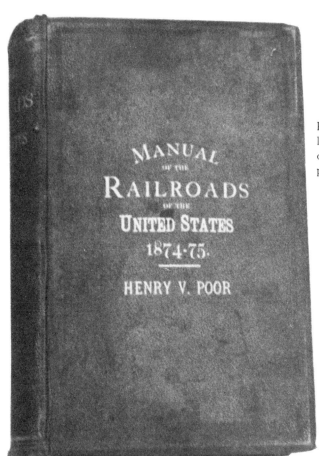

Poor's *Manuals* have beautiful detailed engravings of the steam locomotive and contain a detailed account of the history and operations of all railroads of the times. These manuals are a prize to have on the bookshelf.

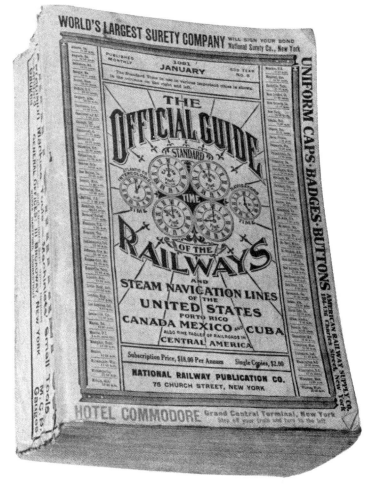

The *Official Railway Guides* are considered to be the bible of the railroadiana collector. These have been in publication since 1867 and copies from the steam era are much in demand today.

Railroad publications of the early 1900s are highly collectible. Here are a few. *Locomotive Engineers Journal*, 1920; *Locomotive Firemen's and Enginemen's Magazine*, 1918; and *Railway Carmen's Journal*, 1908.

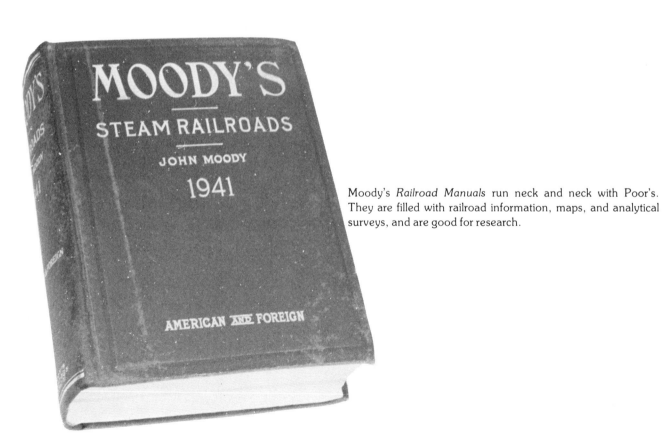

Moody's *Railroad Manuals* run neck and neck with Poor's. They are filled with railroad information, maps, and analytical surveys, and are good for research.

Railway Engineering and Maintenance Cyclopedias are authoritative manuals on the construction and maintenance of the railroad's fixed property. They are profusely illustrated and a must on the railroad bookshelf.

Locomotive Cyclopedias tell everything there is to know about the steam engine and are loaded with definitions of their parts and equipment. Those from the steam era again rate high on the list.

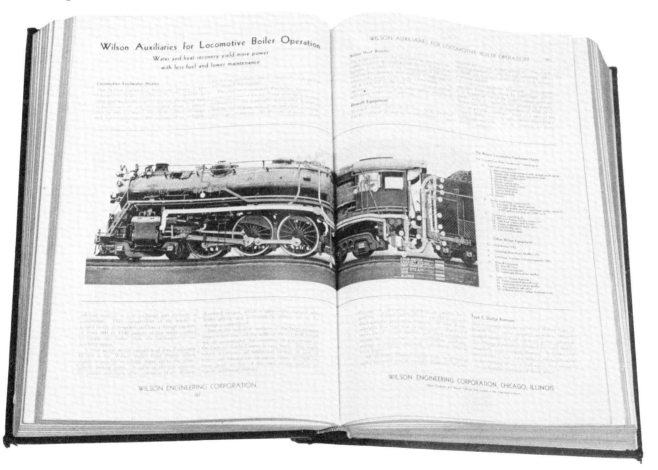

The collector today has a good opportunity to build up a library of railroad books for himself from early editions to the present.

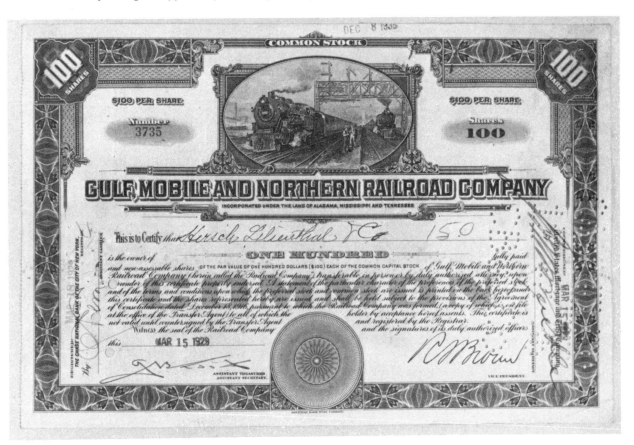

Gulf, Mobile and Northern Railroad Company common stock certificate, 100 shares, dated 1929, with an engraving of a locomotive scene. Many of these stock certificates are works of art.

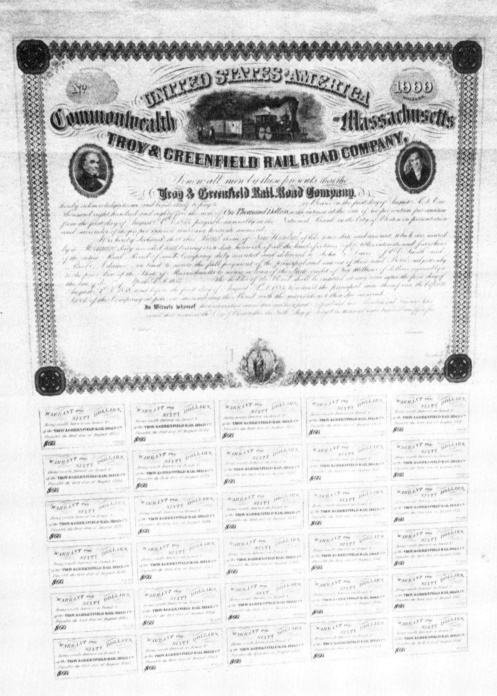

Early railroad bonds contained fine steel engravings of intricate designs and locomotive scenes. Here is a mint $1,000 bond with all the coupons intact. Below it are three redeemed gold mortgage bonds.

Early railroad paper currency, with fine examples of the interesting engravings of locomotives and artwork of the times.

A typical builder's photo taken by an official railroad photographer whose name appears on the bottom of this excellent shot of a locomotive built by the Manchester Locomotive Works in the 1890s.

MANCHESTER LOCOMOTIVE WORKS,
MANCHESTER, N. H.
W. G. C. KIMBALL, Photographer, CONCORD, N. H.

A handsome steam engine named the Highland Light was built at the Taunton Locomotive Co., Taunton, Massachusetts. This accurate lithograph, elaborately done, is an excellent example of these beautiful old builder's lithographs.

An original Currier & Ives lithograph depicting an express train of the 1860s. Their likenesses of the Iron Horse were often more picturesque than accurate.

67

Rare lithograph, circa 1844, showing a primitive steam engine of the times.

An original etching of the New York, New Haven and Hudson River Railroad station in Springfield, Connecticut, by Geo. S. Payne, 1891.

A charming old colorful print of a Lake Shore and Michigan Southern Railway passenger train, with a cornerpiece showing an earlier flyer.

A black-and-white engraving from a page of *Harper's Weekly*, hand colored by the author, *The 9:45 Accomodation Train*. These engravings of railroad scenes from *Harper's Weekly*, Ballou's *Pictorial Drawing Room Companion*, and Frank Leslie's *Illustrated Newspapers* can make a fine print collection.

JULY 4th.

NORFOLK CO. RAIL ROAD.

In addition to the regular **Trains**, a Special **Train** will leave Black-stone at **6¦** o'clock, to accommodate those who wish to witness the

SPLENDID FIRE WORKS
ON BOSTON COMMON.

Returning, will leave Boston at **10¦** o'clock, or immediately after the **Fire Works** are over.

Notice to Dedham Passengers.—This Train will not stop at Dedham.

A discount will be made on **Excursion Tickets** at Blackstone.

Boston, June 29, 1849.   **H. W. NELSON,** *Sup't.*

A rare broadside with a primitive train advertising a Fourth of July fireworks excursion on Boston Common.

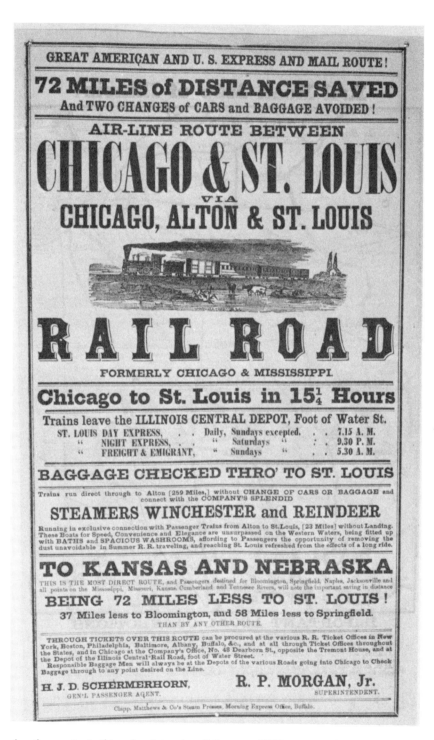

Another rarity is this advertising handbill, circa 1859, put out by the Chicago, Alton & St. Louis Railroad with a cut of an early train. The back side features an interesting map of the railroad line and its connections.

A poster of the 1860s from the Illinois Central Railroad advertising their best farming lands for sale. These posters went everywhere.

Framed original watercolor by Herb Mott, 1961, entitled *A Buffalo Hunt Excursion Train*. Many of his paintings have appeared in books and on the covers of *Railroad* magazine in the days of steam.

An original watercolor by Howard Fogg, dated 1960, entitled *Union Pacific Fast Mail Sherman Hill '55*. Much of his art can be found in the Lucius Beebe and Charles Clegg railroad books.

A colorful Rock Island Railway calendar for 1889, which has survived down through the years—a lucky find.

New York Central Lines calendar for 1925 with the flyleaf still intact over the monthly pages. These are hard to come by in this original condition.

A good way to preserve a railroad calendar is to have it framed to hang on the wall. This Minneapolis & St. Louis Railway calendar for 1945, picturing their roaring freight train, brings back the nostalgic sounds of steam.

An unused Pennsylvania Railroad calendar for 1947. The picture is from a painting by Grif Teller, a noted railroad artist.

Many of these beautiful calendar prints of the steam locomotive are suitable for framing, such as this one from the New York Central Lines 1922 calendar.

Many of the early photographs pictured a broadside view of the Iron Horse, such as this one of the engine Merrimac, with the engineer and fireman standing in the tender. These old photographs help round out the story of the Iron Horse.

The Iron Horse has been kept alive down through the years in photographs. The early photographs of the steam engine are the ones most prized today by the collector. The engineer and fireman posed for this picture.

An original colored photograph, done by the Detroit Photographic Company in 1903, pictures the Twentieth Century Limited of the Lake Shore and Michigan Southern Railroad. Colored old photographs of trains are highly desired by collectors.

Large framed photograph of a Frisco Lines steam engine advertising their fast on-time freight service. These generally hung on the walls of the railroad's business offices.

Framed large colored publicity photo showing scenery along the Louisville and Nashville Railroad's route, made especially for hanging on the walls of depots and ticket offices.

4 Tickets, Please

Tourist Guides and Brochures • Passenger Timetables • Employee Timetables • Passes • Tickets • Postcards • Stamped Envelopes • Pictorial Envelopes • Playing Cards • Stationery • Maps

Like much else in America, railroads right from the beginning ran on paper as well as rails. And "paper" collectibles constitute one vast category that too often is overlooked by collectors, who often seem to myopically zero in on "hardware" in general, and lanterns in particular. We urge you not to overlook the collecting of paper, a grouping that includes tourist guides and brochures, timetables, postcards, and maps, among other items. As for paper—where else could you find such delightful information as this breathless description published in Northern Pacific's 1885 tourist brochure, *The Wonderland Route*, in which a fictitious "Alice" writes from Mammoth Hot Springs Hotel in "National Park," Wyoming Territory: ". . . besides the Rocky mountains and a waterfall—and a big one, too, twice as high as Niagara—there is the grandest old lot of geysers and boiling springs in the world, and a river shut in for several miles of its course by mountains rising hundreds of feet above it, what they call a cañon (pronounced canyon), the walls of which are of such glowing colors that papa said, he could compare it to nothing but the most gorgeous sunset he had ever seen. . . ."

When the railroads began to encourage the American public to travel by train for pleasure, it was the advent of the American tourist, who has been traveling ever since, a drastic departure from earlier days when people rarely, during their entire lifetimes, ventured more than a day's journey from their homes.

The first year after the joining of the rails at Promontory, 150,000 people rode the train between Omaha and Sacramento. By 1890 the travel brochure and tourist guides offered passengers such magnificent inducements that it became a status symbol to cross the continent by train. By 1892, nearly a million had done so.

By 1893, when the last spike of the Great Northern had been driven, five great networks of transcontinental lines crisscrossed the country, and the American traveler could board a train that would take him anywhere in the country he wanted to go, with various railroad companies competing for his travel dollar. Splendid adventure, breathtaking views, luxurious accommodations, gourmet meals, all are glowingly described in tourist guides and brochures aimed at selling the American public on the joys of riding the trains. After all, they were the only game in town. Even miners on their way to the Klondike could choose the all-rail route from San Francisco to Alaska, saving hundreds of miles of ocean travel.

"Paper" adds several dimensions to a railroadiana collection. A large part of the paper you can collect contains pictures that are works of art in themselves, with great charm and, often, delicacy, and the texts graphically recall a vanished way of life. They provide a collector with the historical background or setting for his collection, telling him much of what he should know about the significance and importance of the items he owns, and thereby helping him to better understand and enjoy what he has.

On September 1, 1869, only four months after the Union Pacific and the Central Pacific linked East and West, George A. Crofutt published his first *Guidebook of the Pacific Railroad,* which he titled the *Great Trans-Continental Railroad Guide.* Unfortunately, he was compelled to state in a later guide that "although the name was secured by us on July 22, 1869," it nevertheless was appropriated by a western publisher, who did not stop there, but even stooped to "plagiarizing a great portion of the *Guide.*" As a result, Crofutt changed the name in future editions to *Crofutt's Transcontinental Tourist Guide.*

His third volume, published in 1871, is in my collection. It has an attractive frontispiece showing a covered wagon caravan, the transportation to California in 1849, and two trains coming and going on double tracks, the transportation to California twenty years later. The *Guide* was described as "containing a full and authentic description of over 500 cities, towns, soda and hot springs, scenery, watering places, summer resorts," advising you "where to look for and hunt the buffalo, antelope, deer, and other game; trout fishing, etc.—in fact, to tell you what is worth seeing—where to see it—where to go—how to go—and whom to stop with—while passing over the Union Pacific Railroad, Central Pacific Railroad, their branches and connections, by stage and water, from the Atlantic to the Pacific ocean." Crofutt continued to publish tourist guides down through the years, all of them very collectible today.

However, tourist or railroad guides had been published long before this, as we have seen. The first was published in 1847, and was called *Doggett's United States Railroad and Ocean Steam Navigation Guide.* It contained 132 pages, included maps, and was priced at one shilling. *Harper's New York and Erie Railroad Guide,* published in 1852, contains 136 engravings, which, the guide points out, were intended to be "portraits" of the scenery and objects represented. The text describes the scenery, rivers, towns, villages, and, most important, works on the road. These early railroad guides are filled with fascinating information which is of great interest to the railroad historian.

Harper's *Guide* notes, for instance, that in the time of Britain's Queen Anne, the Assembly of the Colony of New York appropriated £500 to one John Smith and others "for the purpose of constructing a public road leading from New York West, to be constructed within a two year period, wide enough for two carriages to pass, for a distance from 20 to 30 miles." They also were instructed to cut away tree limbs hanging over the tracks to allow carriages to pass beneath. This was to be the beginning of the internal improvement system of the state of New York, but which, as the guide admits, "after 120 years had proceeded no further than to open a canal and two railroads, one completed and the other nearly so, from the city of New York to Lake Erie."

These guidebooks proved so popular that by the 1870s and 1880s a great many publishers had entered the field. A staple of every guidebook was profuse illustrations, including many beautiful engravings of places of interest, such as hotels, resorts, railroad stations, cities, and towns, many of which have long since been torn down. Folded maps, some in color, were often included in the books, and these are of special interest to the collector.

The Pacific Tourist, published by Adams and Bishop in 1880, is described as "the Handsomest Guide Book in the World." Thomas Moran and Albert Bierstadt, both noted painters of the West, contributed rich embellishments and illustrations to the book. *Hittell's Hand-Book of Pacific Coast Travel,* published in 1885, advertises the San Francisco theaters as presenting the latest successes at popular prices, patronized by "the elite of the city"; tailoring made to order in twenty-four hours, with tourist outfits a specialty; Turkish baths; and San Francisco's "Panorama of the Battle of Waterloo," where the "spectator could step at once upon the greatest battlefield of all times." It even includes an advertisement for Freud's Corsets, "the best in the world."

The *Official Northern Pacific Railroad Guide,* published in 1893, is a collector's item. This contains an outline of the Northern Pacific's railroad history since it was chartered in 1864. A book of more than 400 pages, it is filled with picturesque engravings. One of them, *The Dacotah's Farewell to the Buffalo,* is the frontispiece. It shows four Dacotah warriors kneeling over a dead buffalo. The caption, "Go to the Land of the Spirits, we shall soon follow you," may have been an unwitting commentary on the fate of the native Americans as symbolized by a train wending its way across the distant prairies.

Evidently the original owner carried this guide with him in his travels. His penciled notations, a special bonus for me as a collector, were found on many scenes. On the view of the Tacomah Hotel in Tacoma, Washington, he wrote "A lovely view across the Sound—Mt. Tacoma looks so near," and beside the description of Wadena, Minnesota, he wrote, "Pretty place—telephone and eletric lights!"

The 1876 Philadelphia Centennial brought thousands by train to see the great exhibition. Most of them had left home for the first time since homesteading, but trains now could take anyone virtually anywhere and the next seventy years would be the golden years of the railroad.

The tourist guides of the early years soon developed into advertising brochures, designed to sell the American public on the joys of riding the train. George Pullman had provided the railroads with his sleeping cars, reclining chair parlor cars, and palace dining cars; Fred Harvey and his Harvey girls had provided decent food; and plush furnishings, with clean linen, were standard operating equipment. Tourist attractions and places of interest along the routes began to be highlighted in the tourist guides and brochures, and many included a pictorial map pinpointing these scenic marvels.

An especially colorful brochure, the Union Pacific's *A Glimpse of the Great Salt Lake,* was published in 1894. A lady traveler is shown on the cover, dressed in the latest of fashions and carrying her portmanteau and umbrella. The brochure is profusely illustrated with original sketches by Alfred Lambourne, a well-known Salt Lake City artist. It is crammed with information designed to lure "the tourist, pleasure and health seeker, investor, settler, sportsman, artist and the invalid." Besides all that, it also carries a map of the Union Pacific's "World Pictorial Line."

The Northern Pacific's *Wonderland* booklets each contained more than 100 pages. Published annually in the early years of the twentieth century, they were available to anyone sending a six-cent stamp to the line's passenger department. The booklets are collector's items today. Beautifully illustrated with half-tones, they tell all the early history of the land traversed by the railroad from the Great Lakes to Puget Sound. An earlier booklet, published in 1893 by the Northern Pacific, and called *6000 Miles through Wonderland,* is filled with rare photographs taken by the famous F. Jay Haynes, the Northern Pacific's official photographer.

In 1907, to inaugurate its service from Minneapolis to Spokane,

Although now antique, these toy trains fulfilled many a child's Christmas dream.

Candy containers in the shapes of locomotives were made in all sizes. Occasionally they are found with their original candy pellets intact.

Occupational shaving mugs featuring the locomotive were originally the property of railroad engineers and firemen.

This ceramic train, complete with holes for candles and pegs to be stuck into a cake, made some child's birthday a happier one.

Tin advertising sign for Altoona Beers shows two locomotives on Horseshoe Curve, a spot that has always been a favorite of railroadiana photographers and painters.

In the early 1900s, the Travelers Insurance Company gave away many advertising items featuring the train, an example being this colorful pocket mirror.

"Casey Jones," a perennial favorite, is just one from a collection of old sheet music with railroad lyrics.

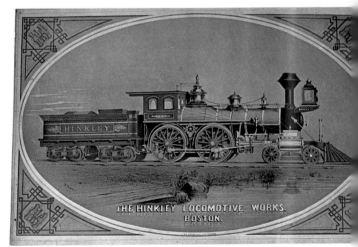

Early builders' lithographs were accurate representations of Iron Horses as they rolled out of the shops. The lithograph above features a locomotive of the Hinkley Locomotive Works, Boston.

Currier & Ives original lithograph, *The Express Train*, is number one in the Best Fifty Small Folio series. All of the early Currier & Ives lithographs featuring trains are fast disappearing and are very collectible today.

This original watercolor by Helmut Kroening is dated 1924 and depicts the Great Northern Railway's William Crooks and a giant ghost train of the future.

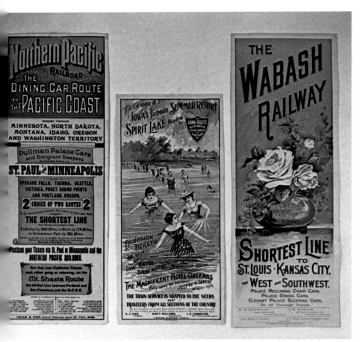

In colorful advertising posters, the railroads featured Pullman palace cars, emigrant sleepers, resort hotels complete with bathers, and even an elegant vase of roses to catch the public's eye.

Not many of the pre-1900 railroad calendars can be found today. To find this 1887 calendar of the Chicago, Rock Island and Pacific Railway is a collector's dream.

The Great Northern Railway published a series of calendars in the 1920s and 1930s featuring the Blackfoot Indians of Glacier National Park.

Northern Pacific Railway's travel brochure of the 1890s, "The Wonderland Route to the Pacific Coast," lured eastern tourists to Yellowstone Park and the Pacific Northwest.

Northern Pacific Railway timetables are of historical interest today. The 1880 timetable shows the line completed to Bismarck, North Dakota. By 1883 it had reached Wallula, Washington Territory, and by 1887 it was complete to Seattle, Tacoma, and Portland.

This group of colorful and picturesque annual passes was issued before the turn of the century.

Playing cards, issued by the railroads, are high on the list of collectibles. Those picturing the steam locomotive and the famous name trains are especially desirable.

Many early greeting postcards—birthday, valentine, and other holidays—used the train motif.

A variety of postage stamps featuring the train were issued by the United States and other countries. The earliest United States stamp, the blue three-cent of the 1869 series, shows a steam locomotive of that era.

Many travelers brought their dining car menus home with them as a memento of their trip.

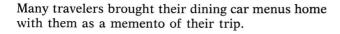

The Missouri Pacific Railway had popular service plates. The Sunshine Special or steam plate was followed by the Texas Eagle diesel plate. Both are favorites with collectors, the diesel the more difficult to find.

Nothing gave the traveler more pleasure than eating in the diner. The array of fine china, shining silver, and gleaming glassware improved the appetite.

In the 1920s and 1930s, the Great Northern Railway's youthful diner used a child's set, consisting of plate, bowl, and cup, decorated with colorful animal characters.

The brass spittoon got a lot of use when tobacco chewing was popular. It was a must in every railroad's depot, diner, waiting room, and smoking car. This one is marked Soo Line on the bottom.

Through the years children's books used the railroad as a theme and captured the imagination of many an American child.

Not too many years ago these cigarette lighters were widely used, but they are not easy to find today.

A builder's plate was affixed to every locomotive, identifying the builder, the location, the year of completion, and displaying a serial number.

Coat lapel emblems and pins that were worn by roalroad men are both interesting and colorful.

A railroad man's watch was his pride and joy. Worn on a gold chain across the vest or on a leather strap hanging from his pants pocket or in the engineer's overall pocket, it helped him to keep the trains running on schedule.

These old kerosene switch stand lamps with their colored targets are now relics of the past.

Locks and keys have always been popular from the early days of railroading. The brass switch lock and switch key are at the top of the collector's list.

The railroads used wax sealers until after World War II, when they were discontinued. Many ended up in the back of a station agent's desk drawer.

Washington, the Soo Line put out a lovely brochure entitled *By Way of the Canyons,* informing the traveler that he had no choice but to take the Soo Line through the great Mississippi valley of Minnesota, into the Dakotas "where the crops never failed," through western Canada where the "grasses grew finer," into the big game country, and the eternal snows of the Rockies.

The entire booklet, also beautifully illustrated, is replete with such extravagant phrases. Who could resist so eloquent a plea, especially when the Soo Line added its famous slogan, "See Europe if you will, but see America first."?

One of the earliest travel brochures in my collection is *The Tourist Guide to the Great Northwest,* published in 1887 by the Central Iowa Railway. It has pictures of lakes and lovely resort hotels, most of them long since torn down, as well as early advertising of railroad lines that are no longer in service.

The Lehigh Valley Railroad brochure, *In Three States,* no doubt is this early also, but it is not dated. This contains many beautifully done small watercolor reproductions of scenery along the route, and on the back cover is a little girl in her pinafore holding an hourglass, with the caption, "The Lehigh runs on TIME."

With an admirable lack of modesty, the booklet declares that "for picturesqueness and variety of scenery, smoothness of roadbed, abundance of convenience, and everything that goes into making traveling a pleasure, this route is unsurpassed. A finer, richer, more inspiring view of mountains, hills, valleys and waterfalls in all their natural grandeur cannot be seen from a car window." What more could a traveler ask?

Another beautiful brochure was put out for the 1902-1903 season by the Santa Fe. It advertised the line's California Limited as offering "every comfort, luxury and safeguard known to modern railway travel." Other Santa Fe brochures advertised the trip to California to be "as easy as going downtown." And still another reads, "Involved in your decision to see the Land Where Every Month is June, is the question: What is the best Limited train to take? That admits only one answer: The California Ltd."

But it would be difficult to surpass the flowery phrases of the New York Central's Hudson River brochure, which seems to be the ultimate in its extravagant description of the river: "Generation after generation have traveled up and down its broad bosom. The Indian in his bark canoe found it an easy highway. Early explorers mistook it for a short route to India. The first settlers found it a friend in their trading ventures, and no history of Revolutionary days is complete without mention of it. Today a fleet of passenger trains ply up and down its banks in all seasons and in all weather. Every scene and every mood of the great river lie like an open book before the traveler."

Not to be outdone, the Great Northern advertised its Oriental Limited as "taking you through the very quick of the northwestern empire, through its cities, farms and forests, over its mountain passes and across its plains, into its past, its present, and its future." All this, in the line's lovely *Seven Sunsets* guide. The centerfold consists of a map that shows not only the route of the train but also where each of their trains would be at sunset each day along the route. According to this ingenious little map, no sun ever set without a Great Northern train sitting in the depot of some city along the line.

This booklet, written by Grace Flandrau, is filled with the highlights of the Oriental Limited's seventy-hour trip from the Great Lakes to Puget Sound. To quote:

> The day's journey has been through a region of almost perfect rural beauty—a scene, which, although you are seeing it for the first time, you have always felt, always known. Farms, farms, farms; rolling hills under the faint sweet blue of a spring sky; under the misty gold of a spring sun; budding groves of oak and maple; bright carpets of winter wheat acidly green; feathery sprouts of corn in endless even rows; the flame of leafless willow hedge like prairie fire along the fields.
>
> The prairie—if the sweet, empty sound of the word signifies, as it seems to, grassy sweeps of untenanted plains—has vanished with the stagecoach and the frontier. Everywhere are villages, towns, and thriving cities. Tall grain elevators stand like towers along the right of way. Fashionable henna colored pigs graze in highly becoming pastures of spring green. Cattle, without their usual display of nervous energy, stare over the landscape like the oil painted cows in our grandmothers' parlors. The sunset light is rosy on the white faces of churches and handsome schools. Only when the eye follows the distances which continually beckon, does a sense of what is gone return. . . .
>
> In the seat beside me a small boy repeats over and over again: "When do the cowboys begin? When do the cowboys begin?" For to this country belonged those glamorous figures, dearer than all others to the youth of the world. And still belong, for although agriculture has invaded Montana, it has not yet completely conquered it. There are cattle ranchers still, and bronco busters with high-heeled boots, and silver spurs, and even six-shooters—although it is considered effeminate to use them. Then at last the cowboys do begin.

The railroads were also scrambling not just for the wealthy travelers but also for passengers who rode "tourist" in an era when classes of travel accommodations were rigidly observed. The Rock Island System's booklet, *Across the Continent in a Tourist Sleeping Car*, advertises its tourist accommodations as "first class in everything but name."

"While the majority of the people who patronize the tourist sleeping cars do so from motives of economy," the brochure gravely declares, "it is a fact that thousands of travelers go tourist because they prefer it. They like the atmosphere of sociability, which is always the rule, and they realize that for cleanliness and comfort, they would fare no better if they paid twice as much."

The great name trains, the dome cars, new equipment, the change from steam to diesel, are all highlighted in the tourist guides and brochures, and all are invaluable to the collector today.

The terms *timetable* and *train* are synonymous today, but it was not always thus. In the early years, it was the newspaper that as often as not published the departure times of the trains—note, the *departure*, not the *arrival*. Early time schedules did not mention the dubious arrival time. It is believed that America's first railroad timetable was carried in the *Baltimore American and Commercial Advertiser* on May 21, 1830, and announced that on May 24 "a brigade, or train of coaches, will leave the Company's Depot on Pratt-street at 7 A.M., 11 A.M., and 4 P.M., and will leave Ellicotts' Mills at 9 A.M., 1 P.M., and 6 P.M.." This was pulled by one horse and the "brigade" was one coach!

The *American Railroad Journal and Advocate of Internal Improvements*, dated Saturday, July 4, 1835, carried this interesting time schedule from the Paterson and New York Railroad Line:

Summer Arrangement for 1835

Passengers will leave Paterson at:
6-½ o-clock A.M. by Steam
10-¼ o-clock A.M. by Steam
2-½ o-clock A.M. by Horses
5-¼ o-clock A.M. by Steam
6-½ o-clock A.M. by Horses

New York, by Jersey City Ferry at:
5-½ o-clock A.M. by Horses
8 o-clock A.M. by Steam
11/12 o-clock A.M. by Steam
3 o-clock A.M. by Horses
6-½ o-clock A.M. by Steam

Passengers with tickets will have a preference in seats.

As the ferry boats do not leave New York precisely at the above times, it is recommended to passengers to procure their tickets and to be at the Ferry a few minutes before the stated hours of departure.

The first timetables issued were just that—a table listing the time the train arrived and departed. It was printed on a single piece of paper or on a card called, quaintly, the "Arrangement of Trains," and usually would be posted on a convenient wall. An 1840 timetable warned: "Passengers should be at the Station at least Ten Minutes before the advertised time of starting."

The train and its schedules seemingly were not on speaking terms for many years. No type of communication existed between train and station. The result, of course, was that train schedules were scarcely, if ever, accurate. A story has been told of William Ogden, president of the Galena and Chicago Union Railroad. In 1848, the Chicago passenger depot had a small tower built on top of its second story. About the time he thought the train was due to arrive, Ogden would climb the stairs to the tower and mount watch with his telescope. He could see five miles out across the prairie. When he saw the train off in the distance, he would shout down the news of its approach to the people waiting in the station.

There is a very interesting early timecard of the Vermont Central Railroad dated July 23, 1849. It lists the arrival and departure of the road's two passenger trains on the run from Montpelier to Windsor and states, without equivocation, that "all freight and irregular trains will keep out of the way of the passenger trains." There is more: "The conductor of the first passenger train down will leave his passenger and baggage car at Windsor and take the cars of the first up train to W. R. Junction, and then attach to his train the cars from the Northern road. The conductor of the second passenger train down will switch off one passenger and baggage car at W. R. Junction and then proceed to Windsor where he will deliver the rest of his train to the Sullivan conductor, then attach his engine to the cars which were left by the conductor of the first train down." One can only trust that this made sense to the switchmen.

In the same year, the timetable of the New York and Erie Railroad stated, "No train will be allowed under any circumstances to leave a station before the time specified on the table, as regulated by the clock at the Piermont office." Many of these early timetables contained woodcuts of the trains of the period. These now are rarities among timetables, and they are of great interest to the historian, as well as to the collector.

As the railroads grew and expanded, timetables began to take on a different appearance. By the 1850s there were railroads in twenty-five of the existing thirty-two states, with New York leading in miles of track. It was something of a hybrid of a transportation system, however, since stagecoaches still were in use and many a timetable contained somewhat cryptic instructions for meeting stagecoaches out where the rails ended. The single-sheet timetable was enlarged and printed on both sides and folded into a pocket-size leaflet. Usually it had a map on one side and the train schedules on the other. Advertising began to appear on them. The pocket timetable of the Erie Railway for 1872 features an ad for Merchant's Gargling Oil on the backside. The Erie sought this type of advertising for their timetables, stating, "Applications for advertising space on these Time Tables should be made to the Ticket Agents of the Company." It also contained the words of the famous Stephen Girard, who, it seems, had learned that it paid to advertise: "I have always considered advertising, liberally and long, to be the great medium of success in business, and prelude to wealth. And I have made it an invariable rule, too, to advertise in the dullest times, as well as the busiest, long experience having taught me that money thus spent is well laid out; as by keeping my business continually before the public, it has secured me many sales that I would otherwise have lost." To all of this, the Erie adds: "If Mr. Girard had lived to the present time, he would have added: *'Advertise in the Pocket Time Table of the Erie Railway.'*" Many of the early timetables contained blank spaces that had not been taken by the advertisers.

Before long, however, the railroads swung into the spirit of promotion, and began to advertise themselves, rather than others. The Pennsy's timetable, dated January of 1877, contains five pages extolling the virtues and superiority of their trains, "running over 100 miles without break or detention of any kind, carrying their supply of fuel with them and taking water from track tanks as they go, a feat not attempted on another line in America or Europe."

The timetable has another interesting paragraph: "The Standard Time of the Pennsylvania Railroad (given on the within tables) from New York to Pittsburgh is Philadelphia local time, which is five minutes slower than New York time, and 19 minutes faster than Pittsburgh time"—a problem which the railroads would not solve until Railway Standard Time was put into effect in 1883.

By the time the trains began to travel across the continent, the nationwide telegraph system was firmly established, and trains could wire ahead their speed and progress to stations along the line; station operators also could wire the next station with the time of the train's arrival and departure. This meant that something resembling accurate scheduling was possible for the first time and connections could be made on time. Thus it became necessary to add more and more pages to the timetables, and gradually they became the standard size four-by-nine-inch pamphlet they are today.

The very early timetables are of course rare and difficult to find. Those from the 1870s, 1880s, 1890s, and early 1900s represent the years when the railroads played a dominant role in the American scene. Very collectible, but also difficult to find, these timetables, among other things, report on the improvements which were being made each year as trains became larger, faster, more beautiful, more luxurious. A growing number of pictures were included of elegantly appointed dining cars, comfortable reclining-chair cars, and the new Pullman Palace sleeping cars.

In 1878 the Chicago, Burlington and Quincy Railroad's timetable advertised the Pullman Palace dining car as "an eating house on wheels, an elegant restaurant within a car—just think of it—eating leisurely at a table d'hote while traveling at the rate of 35 miles an hour. Ten years ago this would have been considered an impossibility—the difference between this and lunch stations with '10 minute bolting' can be appreciated only by those who have experienced it!" And all of this for only seventy-five cents.

Further, this was "the only route running the Pullman Sixteen Wheel drawing room-sleeping car in America, where the passenger obtains the luxury of a drawing room by day and the comforts of a clean and neat bed by night while speeding onward at 30 or 35 miles an hour."

External improvements also were being reported for the benefit of the sober-minded traveler with a scientific bent. In its 1882 timetable, the Lake Shore and Michigan Southern Railroad announced that "no line on this continent has a more permanent and substantial roadway, iron bridges, steel rails and double track."

A common remark, the timetable reports, of those who rode these trains was, "How pleasant and comfortable the Lake Shore Route is. It has all the modern appliances, its equipment is superb, and having no ferry transfers to contend with, *its trains run on time.*"

A special notice is added: "Parties desiring to send for their friends or relatives in the Old Country, by applying can purchase Through Tickets from any point in Europe to this coast at lower rates. We have an Agent in Castle Garden, New York, who will pay particular attention to Emigrants on their way through. In case the parties for whom the tickets have been purchased do not come, the money will be refunded."

Many timetables are collected today for the beautiful pictures that they, like the guidebooks, have of landmarks long since gone. The Lake Shore and Michigan Southern's timetable for 1890 has pictures of three depots: the Lake Shore's passenger station in Chicago, the city's finest and most commodious passenger station at that time; the Grand Central station in New York; and the 138th Street Station, also in New York, built to serve the city's Harlem section. The pictures are of interest because they record the types of engines and equipment used down through the years, with their many changes and improvements. For instance, locomotives lost their diamond stacks and were replaced by a straight, tall smokestack which gradually was shortened.

Timetables during these years often published instructions for the emigrant passenger. The Northern Pacific's 1883 timetable announces that "emigrants to Oregon and Washington Territory go by emigrant trains from St. Paul and Minneapolis to the Pacific coast. The cars composing these trains are fitted with berths similar to the first-class sleepers, having lower and upper berths, the only material difference being that the former are not upholstered. No extra charge is made for berths in these sleepers but passengers furnish their own blankets and such other bedding as they may require."

To reach San Francisco from Portland, passengers took steamers of the Pacific Coast Steamship Company. While first-class passengers "enjoyed all the delicacies of the season," steerage passengers were furnished with "an unlimited supply of good, wholesome food." Whatever that meant.

The Northern Pacific's timetable, dated 1880, stated: "The Line is completed and in operation to a point 61 miles west of Bismarck. Passengers will be carried to 'end of track' as fast as road is in shape for trains." There must have been those who wondered, as they waited, just when that would be.

The Northern Pacific's timetable dated September 1883, covered the opening of its transcontinental line on September 11. As promotional literature, it is all things to all men, wooing the aspiring capitalist with promises of safe investments; would-be manufacturers with descriptions of boundless opportunities in the new cities and towns springing up along the route; miners with promises of gold and silver in the Montana mines; mechanics with the promise of high wages and an abundance of work; laborers with never-ending employment; stockmen with unlimited western grasslands; tourists with the beauty and grandeur of western scenery; and sportsmen with the abundance of game. Professional men, the timetable points out; would have a practice that would grow as towns and cities grew out of the scores of settlements along the route.

By the 1890s the trains went everywhere, the people rode them everywhere they went, and everywhere they went was profusely illustrated in the railroad's timetables. Advertising copy began to undergo a marked change. Instead of stressing their fine equipment, luxurious accommodations, convenience, and safety, the railroads sensed that the public's interest had departed from the purely utilitarian. This was part of the growing-up of the country and of the advent of an era of relative stability and affluence. People could allow themselves to think of pleasure, and the railroads sensed this. Now timetables began to stress, instead, the picturesque land through which their lines ran.

The Baltimore and Ohio advertised itself as "the picturesque B & O." Railroads announced that they were serving such resorts as Saratoga, New York, and Newport, Rhode Island. The 1893 Nickel Plate Road timetable advertised the "world-famous Chautauqua" as being easily accessible by their line, and further suggested that after visiting the 1893 World's Fair, travelers should see Niagara Falls and the famous suspension bridge. The Maine Central Railroad announced itself as "the direct route to and from the summer resorts of Maine."

The peak of railroad travel in America was during the first two decades of the twentieth century. "See America First," the phrase coined by the Soo Line, became the country's byword. Railroad timetables began to promote personally conducted excursions with special rates. The trains also played an important part in the development of America's national parks. The Great Northern featured summer tourist fares to Glacier National Park, advertised the park on its timetables, and used the Rocky Mountain goat as part of its logo. The Indians of the Northwest were also used in the road's railroad advertising.

The Northern Pacific has the same association with Yellowstone National Park. Before the mammoth caves of Kentucky became a national park, the Louisville and Nashville Railway had trains serving the area. Eastern lines carried tourists to the historic sites associated with the nation's founding, and western lines carried tourists to the sites along the nation's new frontier.

These were the years of the luxurous crack trains, complete with beauty parlors, maids, barbershops, and valets. A new idea had been developed, also: a fast train that would make only a few special stops, would travel at high speeds, and would command a premium fare. Hence the frequent use of the word *Limited*, and where once steam engines bore such names as The West Point, The Highland Light, or The William Crooks, now a new sophistication had surfaced. This was the era of the Twentieth Century Limited, The Empire State Express, The Broadway Limited, The Empire Builder, The Olympian, The Super Chief, The Orange Blossom Special, The Oriental Limited, The Aristocrat, and many others.

Timetables from these years and into the 1930s featured these luxury trains. The pictures showed the beautiful steam engines and the elegant passenger accommodations, and they are much sought after by the collector. With the advent of the diesel, timetables lost their appeal for many collectors, although those of the early diesel years are now becoming more and more collectible. As the railroads cut back on their passenger service, fewer timetables were printed. Today, Amtrak timetables are available.

Employee timetables were printed for the use of the railroad employee and the government only, and were entirely different from the public timetables. They contained special instructions and restricted information. The railroads' *Book of Rules* defines an employee timetable as "the authority for the movement of regular trains subject to the rules. It contains the classified schedules of trains with special instructions relating thereto." Most of the information in them is undecipherable to those unfamiliar with the symbols given in the *Book of Rules*. Employees were asked to destroy each timetable as soon as they received their new issues. As might be expected, these are not commonly found, and many collectors consider these to be much more choice than public timetables because fewer were printed and so many destroyed. Some collectors specalize only in the employee timetable.

In 1849, John Wilkinson, president of the Syracuse and Utica Railroad, was so disturbed by the number of persons getting free rides on his train, that on July 1 he instituted a rule that the "only persons allowed to 'pass free' would be the officers and men in the service of the company." This no doubt was the origin of the "pass" as we know it today—the railroads' custom of issuing passes good for free rides on their passenger trains. They most often were given to employees and officials, to the envy of their friends and neighbors. To be able to ride "free" on the trains was one of the status symbols, but the process of doing so was rather complicated.

The employee's name and occupation were written on the front of the pass, and a railroad executive signed it at the bottom, above his printed title. The back carried a printed set of conditions for using the pass, and the receiver, by signing it, agreed to follow them. After the pass was countersigned by still another official, the train's conductor would honor it.

Passes are sought by many collectors and make up another interesting category of railroadiana. Various types of passes were issued. An "annual" pass could be used at any time during the specified year. A "trip" pass was good for a single trip only during as specified time. Employees frequently traveled on "time" passes which were similar to trip passes. Because these generally were picked up by the conductor, they are not as plentiful as annual passes. Upon request, "courtesy" or "complimentary," or "exchange" passes, as they were variously called, were issued to officials of other railroads or to newspapermen, politicians, and members of the clergy. These were issued either for a year, for a specific time, or for a particular trip, as indicated on the pass. Passes given to the clergy were at one-half of the regular fare.

The early passes were made of cardboard and they varied in size. Employee passes often were larger and generally were made on thin paper stock, and they were quite plain in appearance. Soon, however, a standard size came into use. Those dated in the 1860s are extremely rare and difficult to find. Those from the 1870s are also very collectible, and they are now over 100 years old. Many of the railroads listed on these early passes are no longer in existence; they merged with the larger roads many years ago.

An early complimentary pass dated 1865, in my collection, shows a charming funnel-stack locomotive on the face, and has the following on the back: "To Conductors: If this pass is presented by any other person than the one whose name it bears, and the party has not signed the following contract, the conductor will take it up and collect fare. [signed] Isaac H. Sturgeon, Pres't. & Sup't." Below this: "In consideration of this pass, I assume all risk of injuries by accidents, and expressly agree, that the Company shall not be liable, under any circumstances, for any injury to my person, or any loss or injury to my property, and I release said Company from all liability to me as a common carrier in using this pass." This was then signed by the receiver of the pass.

Another pass of this same year in my collection also adds: "Conductors will permit holder of this Pass to travel in Ladies' Cars."

A clergyman's pass dated 1883 has the following conditions printed on the back: "It is not transferable, and is only intended for such clergymen residing in the towns on the line of the New York, Pennsylvania and Ohio Railroad, as are settled Pastors and engaged for no part of their time in any other profession or business. It must be shown to the Conductor with the passage ticket, otherwise full fare will be collected."

Passes were always numbered for accounting purposes. While some of the early passes are quite plain, many of the later passes are beautifully engraved, and many also feature picturesque railroad scenes with quaint bridges, trestles, right-of-ways, early engines, and rolling stock. The artwork often was ornate and handsomely done, as was the Atlantic, Mississippi and Ohio Railway Company's 1873 pass which graciously states that "during 1873 the A. M. & O. extends the courtesy of free travel" to the bearer. This pass was made by the Continental Banknote Company of New York, one of the many bank note companies and printers that did this type of work.

Passes of the 1880s through the early 1900s also are much in demand by collectors and are fast disappearing. In fact, any pass up through the 1930s is now being hunted down by collectors. Passes can be collected in a variety of ways: by the yearly dates, by certain railroads, by type of design, by the early trains and railroad scenes pictured on them, or by the type of pass itself. Annual passes are the easiest to find, as they often were saved by their owners. It is surprising how many of them have survived, no doubt kept by the family as a personal memento or because of the railroader's name on them. An added bonus may be a prominent name or signature on one of these early passes. Very rare are the solid silver passes issued by Otto Mears for the Colorado roads he owned. These are in private collections today, and valued in the thousands of dollars.

In 1830 a Baltimore newspaper carried the following advertisement for the Baltimore and Ohio Railroad: "Positive orders have been issued to receive no passengers into any of the cars without tickets." Tickets in those early days were simply large sheets of paper, pieces of cardboard, or metal disks of various sizes. Some railroads followed the custom used in England: When the passenger paid his fare his name was written down in a ledger. The book was then given to the conductor and he used it to check off the passengers.

Purchase of a ticket in those early years might include more than was bargained for. It was not uncommon for passengers to be called upon to help carry water or wood if the train stalled at a lonely spot. Sometimes they even helped push the train up a grade that was steeper than usual. Down through the years, many different types of tickets were used, and a great variety of them are available to collectors today.

I have in my collection a ticket issued by the Chicago and Northwestern Railway which was "Good for one Continuous Emigrant Passage from Reno to Virginia City," dated 1877, subject to the following contract: "In consideration of the reduced rate at which this ticket is sold it will be forfeited if not presented to the Union Pacific RR Co. for passage within eight days from following date: May 7, 1877, which must also be officially stamped on the back. And this contract signed by the purchaser. No stop-over check to be issued on this ticket, and the coupons belonging hereto will not be received for passage if detached from the contract. This ticket is to be exchanged by the Union Pacific RR. Co. at Omaha for one limited to nine days from date of issue on which baggage will be checked to destination only." One Jim Harrington signed this ticket and it was witnessed by O. D. Sloat. One cannot help but wonder how Jim Harrington fared in his new venture, as he made the last portion of his long trip, from Reno to Virginia City, from the east.

Another ticket, dated 1880, issued by the Fitchburg Railroad states: "One First Class Passage, Fitchburg to Rochester, New York. Only upon presentation of this ticket with coupons attached, and not good unless stamped by Ticket Agent. In selling this ticket for passage over other roads, this Company acts only as Agent, and assumes no responsibility beyond its own road, which extends from Boston to Greenfield only.

"Conductors are required to detach from this ticket and take up the coupons over their respective lines. The conductor upon this road at the end of the route will take up the ticket, as well as the coupon, over this road. If the coupons belonging to this ticket are detached, they will not be received for passage."

Since the beginning of rail travel in America nearly 150 years ago, there was no greater excitement for most Americans than buying a ticket to ride on the train. It mattered little whether it was to the next town or across the continent. What they really were buying was a ticket to adventure and excitement, a journey into an undiscovered country, with new faces to see, new things to learn, new wonders to look at, new horizons to discover. If you held that ticket in your hand, it promised you great things to come. Those of us who were obliged to stay at home would try to catch a glimpse of the train as it went by, to see the people at the windows, to envy them, and to hope that some day we, too, would be able to buy a ticket, stand on the station platform, and watch the train slide to a stop, and climb those steps into adventure.

As any collector of postcards showing railroad scenes will tell you, the price of these small pieces of cardboard has been skyrocketing each year, and they are beginning to be hard to find at any price. Wherever postcards may be for sale, whether at the garage sale down the block, or the large antique or stamp dealer's show, the railroadiana collector is there, carefully turning the pages of old postcard albums or shuffling through boxes of postcards, interested only in those having to do with the railroad. If it is his lucky day, he may find one or two at a price he can afford to pay, or buy them at whatever the price, knowing that the next time the price no doubt will be higher.

As railroads began to lure tourists around the turn of the century, picture postcards increasingly were offered for sale at railroad depots and lunchrooms. Who could resist buying them to send to friends and relatives, proof of the wonders they were experiencing? Usually priced at two for a nickel, they could be mailed for a penny, an inexpensive memento of this great event. Thousands upon thousands of postcards were bought and mailed. They pictured the train itself or the depot from which they left, or railroad scenes along the way. Nearly everyone owned a picture postcard album with cards carefully mounted in the corner slots, and a Sunday afternoon could be whiled away looking at them. With today's revival of interest in nostalgia, these reminders of a more tranquil era are once again proving to be of great interest.

Multitudes of postcards having to do with trains and railroads were made by various card manufacturers both here and abroad. The railroads also published their own cards showing locomotives, passenger trains, depots, bridges, and scenes along the right-of-way. A waterfall with the train crossing the bridge above it was a favorite. Runners-up tended to be depots, night or day, with passenger trains coming and going, high trestles with trains on them, or narrow-gauge switchbacks. All of them displayed the railroad's name on the front or back of the card and included a description of the scene. Many collectors are interested only in these. The railroads also had numerous cards made for advertising purposes. These, which they gave away, usually featured their name passenger trains. These also are very collectible. In addition to the single postcards, there were folders of cards which would unfold to show the train, depots, and a set of views along the route.

Many collectors specialize, while others are interested in any card that has anything at all to do with the railroad. Some collect only depots, others bridges and trestles, some only those cards showing the train itself. Postcards featuring train wrecks are both popular and hard to find. Those that were kept in their original albums, or stored in a box in the attic, usually are in excellent condition, but others have been much abused. The undamaged card, with an unsoiled picture, clear message, and clearly readable postmark, is highly prized and most valuable. Some collectors mount their cards in an album displaying the picture side only, while others prefer a special album that allows both sides of the card to show.

As far as is known, the South Carolina Railroad has the distinction of being the first to carry mail. The mail pouch was put onto a railway car pulled by the Best Friend of Charleston in 1831 and it was carried to its destination, 136 miles away. In 1838 President Martin Van Buren signed a bill making every railroad a carrier of the mails. By 1840 the railroads had begun to provide special space and facilities for handling the mail, and by 1845 space "especially fitted up for the accommodation of the mail, and for the assortment of letters and papers on the road" was being furnished by many railroads. As an experiment in speeding up the mail, a car equipped for sorting mail en route was operated on the Hannibal and St. Joseph Railroad in 1862. On August 28, 1864, the first permanent Railway Post Office car for picking up, sorting, and distributing the mail en route was placed in operation by the Chicago and Northwestern Railway on a run from Chicago to Clinton, Iowa.

In the beginning the mail cars were a part of the regular passenger train. The first mail-only train was built for the New York Central Railroad and carried nothing but mail. It ran between New York and Chicago on tracks cleared especially to give it the right-of-way.

In the early days much of the public mail was postmarked with the name of the railroad cancelling the stamp. Route agents traveling on the trains hand-stamped these envelopes, and these cancellations are now very rare. Also during this period the railroads did not use a postage stamp on their own envelopes but instead initialed them R.R.S. (rail-road service) on the corner of the envelope, indicating that the letter was transported by the railroads' mail service. In later years, R.R.B. (rail-road business) was used. Many of these envelopes have the railroads' name printed on the envelope, and some have illustrations of early locomotives. The early illustrated R.R.S. or R.R.B. envelopes are quite scarce.

After the route agents became Railway Post Office clerks, R.P.O. (Railway Post Office) marks began to appear on envelopes carried by railroad post office cars on designated routes. Some envelopes would also have an R.M.S. (Railway Mail Service) mark to cancel the stamp. Many R.P.O. cancellations are found on envelopes dating before 1900, and they are highly collectible and much in demand. The more modern R.P.O. envelopes are quite common. However, since Railway Post Office cars now have been discontinued, R.P.O. cancellations also have disappeared from the scene. In more recent years, a variety of R.P.O. cancellations have been made especially for collectors and these covers can now be found in philatelic shops.

The collecting of the pictorial envelopes used by the railroads is a rare category for the railroadiana collector. The railroads became aware of the advertising potential of these envelopes and the publicity possibilities that they could have. Many showed a typical train of the period. In 1860, the South Carolina railroad used the entire front of the envelope to picture their train. These illustrated envelopes were in general use until the turn of the century. Many other firms also used the illustrated envelope and featured a train, such as the envelope in my collection showing an early train traveling across the face of a Rockford watch. I also have in my collection an envelope from the Rail-road Bank, Decatur, Illinois, dated 1854 and picturing an early train. Another interesting envelope, dated 1895 and used by a stove company, shows a fifteen-car freight train across the entire envelope, advertising the "largest single shipment of oil stoves ever made."

As more and more people began to ride trains and to remain on them for some length of time, card playing became a popular diversion, and playing cards issued by the railroads began to make their appearance. These railroad-marked playing cards make up another category for the railroadiana collector. The early playing cards from around the turn of the century are of special interest. Many of these were souvenir decks in a two-piece cardboard slipcase. The back sides of the cards usually have a design or a picture, while the faces have fifty-two separate photographic views of scenes along the railway's system. The back design is very ornate and generally includes the railroad's logo. Pictures ran heavily to passenger trains or pretty girls. Finding a souvenir deck in its original case, the cards' original gilt finish still on them, or, better still, a mint deck that has never been used, is a collector's dream.

Railroads also issued regular playing cards with standard faces and without pictorial scenes in cardboard cases with folded tops. The Rock Island and the Burlington roads probably were the first to use the joker and the ace of spades for advertising purposes, and these decks, dating from the 1890s, are very collectible. By 1900 the Chicago and Alton Railroad, as well as other roads, also were putting advertising on the jokers. The backs of the cards also were used for advertising. The case, too, featured advertising—usually a name train, or the railroad's logo or slogan, such as the Chicago and Alton's cowboy girl of 1903, and their "only way."

As the years passed, playing cards became more streamlined in appearance, the backs featuring only the railroad's logo. The case usually featured the same logo that was on the cards. Some railroads issued anniversary decks celebrating 100 years of transportation progress, and these are very collectible. The earlier decks, of course, are preferred, along with those from lines no longer in existence. A complete deck with the joker, in its original case, all in fine condition, is a real find for the collector.

Railroad stationery is another category that is highly sought by railroadiana collectors. Early letterheads and envelopes from railroads now defunct often have fancy lettering and charming engravings of locomotives and railroad scenes. Some of the railroads used the backs of their stationery for advertising and many such sheets carried maps. Besides all this, the letter itself often can be fascinating reading. A collection of letters alone would be of much interest.

But there are many related items in this field, too: railroad-marked pens and pencils, rulers, blotters, memo pads, all produced in large quantities with wide distribution. Because so much of this was discarded, these items, and especially those from the earlier years, are scarce today. Among these are early wooden rulers featuring railroad slogans and logos and showing routes of the sytem. Many rulers also were made of tin and celluloid, graduating down to the present-day plastic. Pens and pencils fall into this same grouping, the earlier ones being more interesting in style, and the later ones including today's ball-point pens. However, even these are collectible today with so many railroads slowly leaving the scene. Blotters also have colorful pictures and copy on them. With the advent of the ball-point pen, blotters have virtually disappeared, and thus have become highly collectible. You could put together an interesting collection of stationery-related items, which will increase in value as they disappear from view.

Don't overlook the many interesting maps issued by the railroads down through the years. Large maps showing a railroad's system invariably could be found on the walls of the line's ticket offices and in its depot waiting rooms. Large survey maps hung on the walls of railroad construction offices pinpointing the line as it developed. Roll-down maps featuring railroads were used in classrooms and libraries. When a new line was started, the railroad usually issued a map of the proposed route in order to promote the sale of its stocks and bonds. Union Pacific's first official map was filed with the secretary of the interior's office in 1862. When the actual route was completed in 1869, there was hardly a deviation from the original proposed route. Maps also were printed under the direction of the states' railroad and warehouse commissions, and these would show the railroad lines in the state for the year of publication. Colorful maps promoting land sales along a railroad's right-of-way, pictorial maps advertising tourist attractions, and early maps showing railroads under construction can be found. Many pocket maps were published—large-size maps that folded up in a hard-cover book. Most old books on railroad history have foldout maps showing existing lines as well as those for new lines under construction.

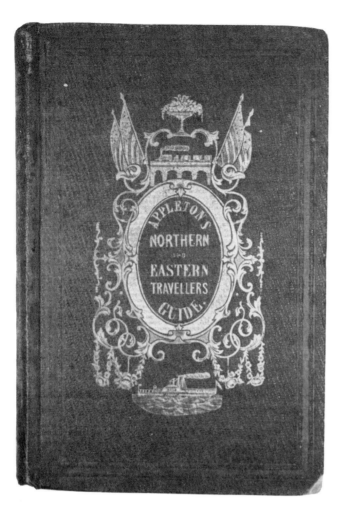

Appletons *Northern and Eastern Traveller's Guide* book, dated 1853, contains over 300 pages of the latest information on the railroads and steamboats then in operation. Thirty steel-engraved foldout maps, and twenty-six steel-engraved illustrations, enhance the value of this book on the early railroad lines in the country at the time.

Crofutt's Trans-Continental Tourists' Guide for 1871. Crofutt's guidebooks were considered by many to be the best and most complete illustrated guidebooks ever published up to that time. It is a most interesting old book to thumb through.

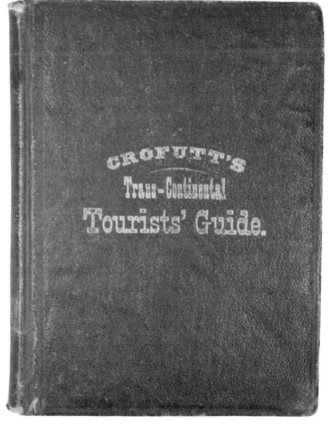

This early illustrated guidebook furnished the traveler with information and illustrations depicting scenes along the route. The frontispiece is an example of the many interesting engravings throughout the book, the prominent feature of this early guide.

William's *Pacific Tourist*, a guide across the continent, is an example of one of the numerous guidebooks that followed Crofutt's first edition in 1869. It is opened to show its interesting frontispiece.

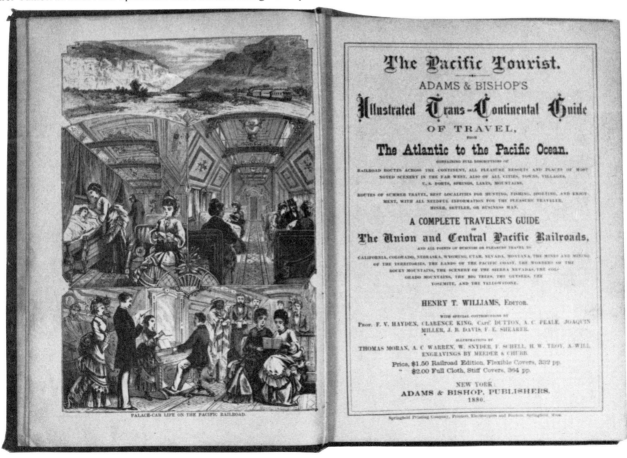

PALACE-CAR LIFE ON THE PACIFIC RAILROAD.

The Pacific Tourist.

ADAMS & BISHOP'S

Illustrated Trans-Continental Guide

OF TRAVEL,

FROM

The Atlantic to the Pacific Ocean.

CONTAINING FULL DESCRIPTIONS OF

RAILROAD ROUTES ACROSS THE CONTINENT, ALL PLEASURE RESORTS AND PLACES OF MOST NOTED SCENERY IN THE FAR WEST, ALSO OF ALL CITIES, TOWNS, VILLAGES, U.S. FORTS, SPRINGS, LAKES, MOUNTAINS,

ROUTES OF SUMMER TRAVEL, BEST LOCALITIES FOR HUNTING, FISHING, SPORTING, AND ENJOYMENT, WITH ALL NEEDFUL INFORMATION FOR THE PLEASURE TRAVELER, MINER, SETTLER, OR BUSINESS MAN.

A COMPLETE TRAVELER'S GUIDE

OF

The Union and Central Pacific Railroads,

AND ALL POINTS OF BUSINESS OR PLEASURE TRAVEL TO

CALIFORNIA, COLORADO, NEBRASKA, WYOMING, UTAH, NEVADA, MONTANA, THE MINES AND MINING OF THE TERRITORIES, THE LANDS OF THE PACIFIC COAST, THE WONDERS OF THE ROCKY MOUNTAINS, THE SCENERY OF THE SIERRA NEVADAS, THE COLORADO MOUNTAINS, THE BIG TREES, THE GEYSERS, THE YOSEMITE, AND THE YELLOWSTONE.

HENRY T. WILLIAMS, EDITOR.

WITH SPECIAL CONTRIBUTIONS BY

PROF. F. V. HAYDEN, CLARENCE KING, CAPT. DUTTON, A. C. PEALE, JOAQUIN MILLER, J. B. DAVIS, F. E. SHEARER.

ILLUSTRATED BY

THOMAS MORAN, A. C. WARREN, W. SNYDER, F. SCHELL, H. W. TROY, A. WILL. ENGRAVINGS BY MEEDER & CHUBB.

Price, $1.50 Railroad Edition, Flexible Covers, 332 pp.
$2.00 Full Cloth, Stiff Covers, 364 pp.

NEW YORK:

ADAMS & BISHOP, PUBLISHERS,

1880.

Springfield Printing Company, Printers, Electrotypers and Binders, Springfield, Mass.

Examples of some of the many pictorial guidebooks travelers used shortly after the driving of the golden spike opening the way west. Their illustrations alone are really worth much more than the price they bring.

The railroads also published their own *Official Railroad Guides* for the tourist. This *Official Northern Pacific Guide* for 1893 is profusely illustrated and has a large foldout map in the pocket of the back cover.

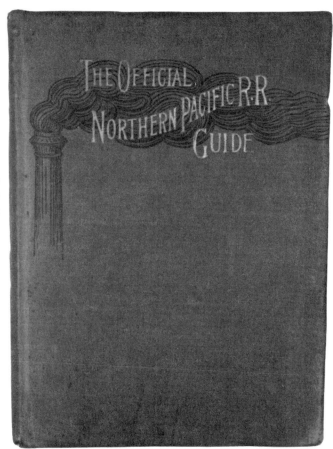

Tourist guide booklets were profusely illustrated and full of information for the tourist traveling by rail. These early examples are rarities.

One of the many charming illustrations contained in these early guidebooks.

Three choice travel brochures of the early 1900s: Great Northern's "Seven Sunsets," New York Central's "Hudson River," and the Soo Line, with the slogan they initiated, "See Europe if you will, but See America First."

Denver & Rio Grande Railroad scenic picture book. These were sold to the tourist at the depot or on the train as souvenirs of the trip.

Some of the Northern Pacific's Wonderland booklets published around the turn of the century beautifully illustrated that era. At one time available from the railroad for a six-cent stamp, these booklets are collector's items today.

Examples of the numerous travel and information folders issued by the railorads down through the years.

A single-sheet timetable of the Harlem Extension R.R. for 1871. These were posted on the depot walls in those days for the public to read.

An early newspaper time schedule of the Paterson and New York Railroad Line listing both steam and horsepower departure time. You had your choice of going by horse or steam power.

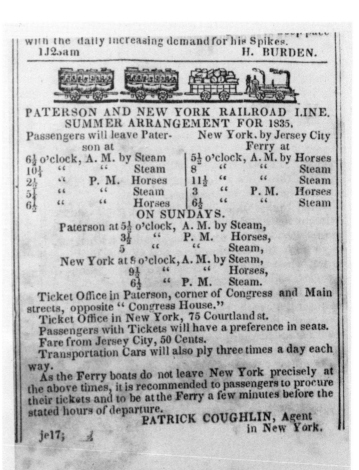

Three early and very rare single-card timetables.

Northern Pacific timetable of 1883 partially unfolded to show the many illustrations and the general information contained in many of these early timetables for the traveler.

A grouping of folded public timetables during the late 1800s with their interesting pictorial covers.

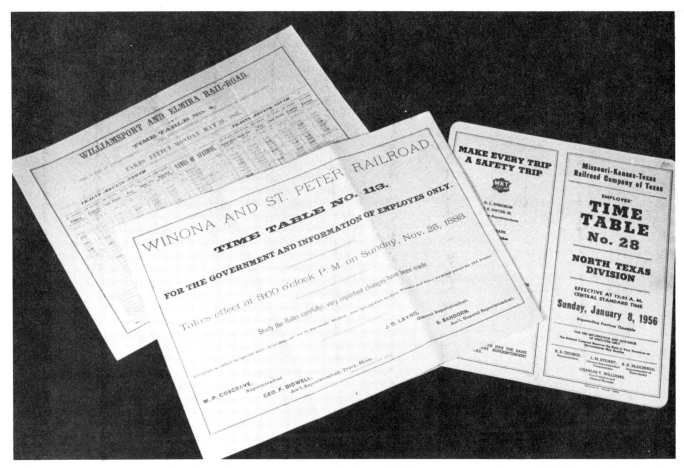

Examples of employee timetables down through the years: single sheet of 1857, large string-tied pages of 1883, and folding booklet type of 1956. These were restricted from public use and the collector has a harder time finding them.

An arrangement of public timetables issued after the turn of the century with their interesting covers. Note the famous Katy on the back side of the 1901 Missouri Kansas Texas timetable.

Examples of early annual passes, which were given out by the railroads for free rides.

Back side of an annual pass showing statement of conditions and signatures validating the pass, leaving the railroad free of all liability.

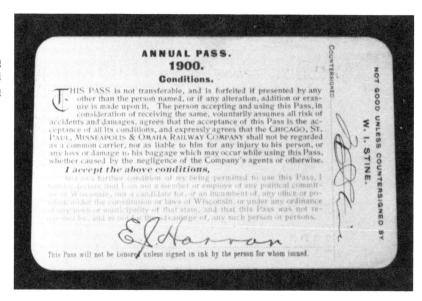

Some early passes were intricately and finely designed. This is a typical example, printed by the Continental Banknote Company of New York.

A grouping of complimentary passes—employee, clergy, transfer, legislative, etc., all of whom were out for a free ride too.

George M. Pullman himself signed this Pullman Palace Car Company pass.

Both sides of an 1882 Lake Erie & Western Railway editor's pass. A railroad pass showing a photo of the bearer is rare.

A ticket box with all its tickets still inside the chutes, rescued from a small-town depot before it was razed. With it are a ticket dater or validator and the conductor's ticket punch.

The railroads had many postcards made for them promoting their name trains and tourist attractions.
These are especially collectible.

A page opened in an album full of railroad postcards collected down through the years by the author.

A set of fifteen postcards was put out by the Baltimore and Ohio Railroad for their 1927 Fair of the Iron Horse at Halethorpe, Maryland. The set originally cost fifteen cents—today it is listed at twenty-five dollars.

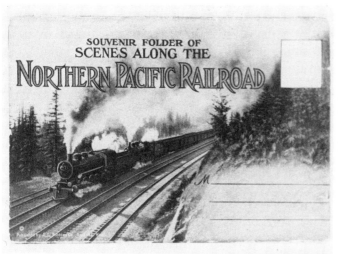

Through the years many postcard folders full of scenes along the route were sold to the traveler at the railroad's depots and lunch counters. These unfolded into a string of cards with pictures on both sides, a pack of postcards all in one, a real bargain.

No stamp, but initials R.R.S. in corner, indicating that this letter was privately carried by the railroad, a common practice of the railroads in the early days. These are also rare.

Envelopes with early railroad postmarks on them are rarities today. Here are some examples.

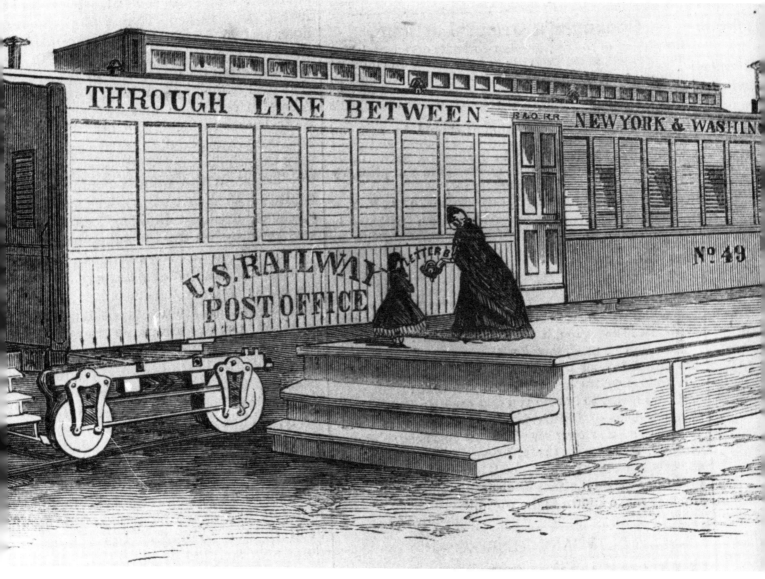

An early engraving from Frank Leslie's *Illustrated Newspaper*, dated 1864, showing the new U.S. Railway Post Office exterior, with box for drop letters.

Postcard dated 1873, with postmark of the Winona & St. Peter Railroad. It pays to look through old postcard albums for cards with railroad or R.P.O. postmarks. You may strike it lucky.

Philatelic covers with their R.P.O. postmarks have become more collectible since the railway post office cars were discontinued.

Pictorial covers with locomotives are very collectible. Here is an interesting one with a train across the entire envelope.

A pictorial cover of the Rockford Watch Company, picturing a train. This paper item may be of interest to the watch collector, too.

Thousands of interesting paper collectibles, such as those shown here, can be found by the collector, all part of the collecting of railroad memorabilia.

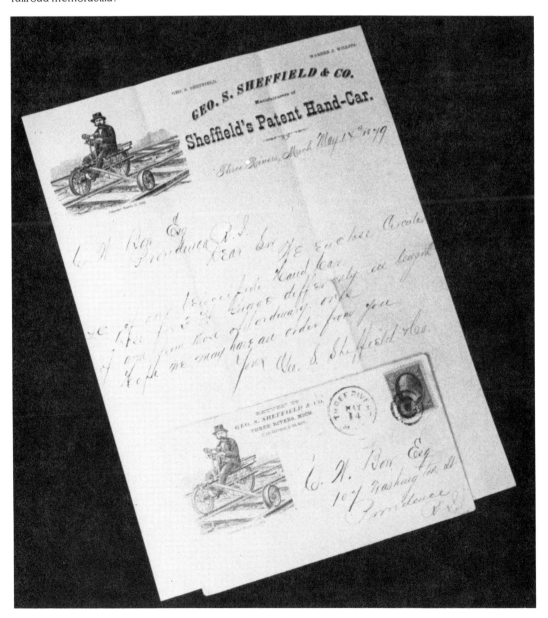

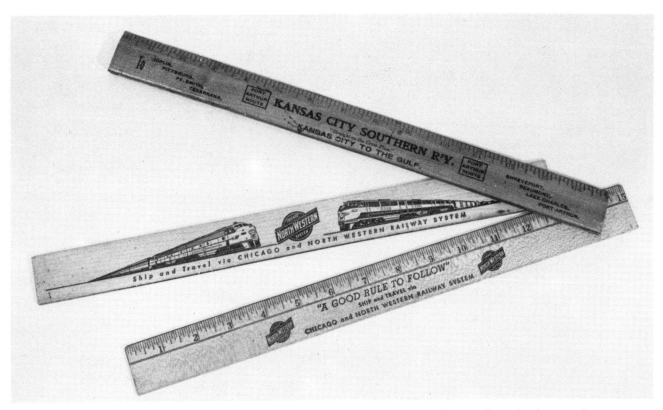

Railroads gave out rulers by the thousands through the years; many of them have wound up in collector's cabinets today.

When the ball-point pen came into style, blotters virtually disappeared. Those given out by the railroads in the past are now sought after.

Railroads also handed out countless numbers of advertising pencils.

There were hundreds and hundreds of all types of maps put out by the railroads and for the railroads, all of which are of interest to the collector.

Many of these large roll-down maps were used in classrooms, libraries, offices, etc., and were good advertising for the railroads.

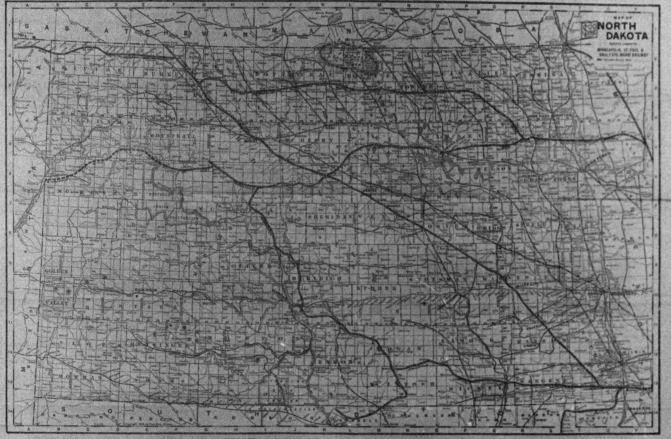

Many railroads issued maps promoting the sale of land along their right-of-way.
This Soo Line map of North Dakota is a fine example.

5 Dinner Is Served

Dining Car Menus • China • Silver • Glassware • Cuspidors • Book Matches • Cigarette Lighters • Ashtrays • Games • Puzzles • Baggage Checks

From the very beginning, riding the train was an adventure, and those who rode, rode into history. What could have been more exciting than sitting behind the De Witt Clinton as it left Albany for Schenectady on that warm day in August of 1831? So many people wanted to make the trip that flatcars equipped with long benches had to be added to the three passenger coaches—builders had not quite got the hang of it and the first coaches they designed looked like stagecoaches on rails. The De Witt Clinton's cars were joined to each other with three-foot-long chains. When the engine began to move, the cars started with a mighty jerk, dumping passengers on the floor, one on top of the other.

Those riding in the rear on the flatcars were in sudden danger of being burned alive as sparks from the wood-burning engine blew about them. Those who had brought umbrellas to shield themselves from the sun used them as protection from the sparks until the umbrellas caught fire and had to be tossed into the grass along the track, setting it on fire, too. But, as passengers took turns beating out small flames licking at their clothing, no one complained or asked for their money back. Apparently they felt the excursion had been thrilling—seventeen miles to Schenectady and back, behind a real steam engine at speeds up to thirty miles an hour—and were willing to sacrifice a few lost umbrellas, burned dresses, and scorched top hats, as well as to endure a few bruises.

It does not require much imagination to see that riding the early trains was a rugged experience, and things did not get better in a hurry. When they did, it was the passengers who brought about the changes. Their complaints at length grew loud enough to be heard. After the excitement and novelty wore off, people still wanted to ride the trains, but they wanted to do so in comfort. The hard, uncomfortable wooden benches running the length of the cars were replaced with rows of seats on either side of a center aisle. Eventually the seats would even be upholstered.

The direct beneficiaries of this demand for comfort are those of us who love railroadiana and collect it. The result of this demand for comfort was the production of a wide range of collectibles designed to appease those growing throngs of people who rode the trains—everything from menus, beautiful china, glassware, and silver used in the dining cars to matchbooks, souvenirs, even spittoons and other smoking accessories. These are glamorous collectibles, eagerly sought today, and they have a colorful history.

Still operating under the influence of the stagecoach era, the first trains stopped for the night, and everyone got out and put up at an inn. Before long, however, trains began to run at night, and passengers spent the night resting as best they could sprawled out on their seats. The cars were lighted with candles—when someone thought about it; often, the passengers brought their own. Next, kerosene lamps lighted the cars, at least for those passengers who sat directly beneath them. And in the winter there was heat from wood-burning stoves.

Between 1830 and 1850, many improvements were made in the name of comfort, as more and more people rode the trains for longer and longer distances. The first sleeping car—the term is used loosely, since sleep was possible only for those in a state of exhaustion—was used as early as the winter of 1836-1837. To many, this was not much of an improvement. It was a makeshift arrangement, a remodeled day coach divided into four compartments. Each compartment had three crudely built bunks, one above the other, along one side of the car, with hard, narrow mattresses. There was no bedding of any kind; passengers covered themselves with their coats and used their carpetbags for pillows. A washbasin, a bucket of water, and a roller towel were provided at one end of the car.

The first sleeping car was put into operation on the Cumberland Valley Railroad between Harrisburg and Chambersburg, Pennsylvania, and it was not long before other lines began experimenting with sleeping cars. In June of 1856, the Illinois Central put six stateroom-sleeping cars into service. Known as Gothic cars, these were nearly fifty feet long and almost ten feet wide.

Had the first sleeping cars offered something resembling comfort, however, one of the great inventions of all times might not have been developed. As he lay awake one night aboard a sleeping car halfway between Buffalo and Westfield, New York, George Mortimer Pullman, a successful Chicago contractor, came to the conclusion that there must be a better way. He began to sketch a plan for a passenger coach with seats that could be converted into beds and berths that could be let down from the ceiling by ropes or pulleys.

In 1859, Pullman converted two Chicago and Alton passenger cars (nos. 9 and 19) at the railroad's shops in Bloomington, Illinois. The seats were immovable and had no springs; a narrow strip of carpeting covered the floor, and ten open sections were crowded into the small, forty-four-foot-long coach. At each end there was a small toilet room, large enough for one person, with a tin washbasin. Windows were a little over a foot square and were set immovably in place. Two small wood-burning stoves furnished heat, and candles furnished light. The first of these cars, No. 9, made its initial trip from Bloomington to Chicago on the night of September 1, 1859, and it was an immediate success.

Encouraged, Pullman stuck to his drawing board. In 1864, he began to build the first Pullman sleeping car, using his own money. He named it the Pioneer and it cost $20,178 to complete—a phenomenal sum in those days. The car had upper berths, which during the day could be folded up against the ceiling. There was space to store ample bedding and comfortable mattresses inside the berth. There were carpets on the floor, black walnut woodwork, ornamental mirrors, and plush upholstered seats. The car was heated by a hot-air furnace under the floor, and lighted with three candles. There were eight sections, two compartments at each end, and a washroom.

There was just one problem: The car was much longer, higher, and wider than the other railroad cars of its day. It measured fifty-four feet long and ten feet wide, and some of the bridges on the Chicago and Alton's line were simply too narrow to allow it to pass; nor could it get past the depot platforms.

Then tragedy played its part. President Lincoln was dead, assassinated at Ford's Theater on April 14, 1865, and the grieving Mrs. Lincoln asked that the Pioneer be attached to the funeral train at Chicago for her use. Bridges were widened and station platforms whittled down so the Pioneer could pass—and after this, all platforms and bridges conformed to this size. Thousands crowded the rail lines to watch the funeral train pass, and thousands saw the Pioneer during the trip from Chicago to Springfield. When the grief and shock had worn off, thousands also realized that they, too, wanted to ride in a Pullman sleeping car.

The Pullman Palace Car Company was organized, and soon first-class passengers were riding in luxurious cars on fine plush seats, which could be converted into snug berths at night. The nation's centennial year of 1876 brought an enormous increase in travel, and by the 1880s and 1890s, passengers were surrounded by all the excesses of the late Victorian years, with plush upholstery, rich carpets, velvet hangings and draperies, hand-carved paneling, and gilt mirrors. The Pullman really was a "palace on wheels." It also was a new word in the English language.

The earliest known instance of meals being served on a train was on January 10, 1853, when the Baltimore and Ohio Railroad hired a caterer to provide food and refreshments for passengers on two special trains the railroad ran from Baltimore to Wheeling, West Virginia, and back to mark completion of the road to that point.

By 1863 the first dining cars were in service on the Philadelphia, Wilmington and Baltimore Railroad between Philadelphia and Baltimore. There were two cars, both of them remodeled day coaches fifty feet long. Each was fitted with an eating bar, steam box, and "other fixtures usually found in a first-class restaurant." Food was prepared at the terminal and put aboard the cars just before they left. They stayed in service for about three years.

In 1867, George Pullman introduced his "hotel car." These were sleeping cars equipped with kitchen and dining facilities. In 1868, he built his first all-restaurant car, which he named the Delmonico in honor of New York's famous restaurant, and it went into operation on the Chicago and Alton Railroad that year. A sumptuous dinner was served for one dollar.

Nothing before or since has brought greater well-being and comfort to the traveler by train than the dining car—with the possible exception of the sleeping car. The dining cars, particularly, represent the golden era of train travel, and one of the great fascinations for railroadiana collectors are the menus.

But, as we read through the lists of sumptuous meals, we must remember that the common man who traveled west of the Mississippi during the years of the late nineteenth century did not dine as well. His particular plight led to another innovative idea. Most passengers traveling west either packed their own lunches or attempted to eat at lunch counters set up in the depots along the way. This became such a hit-and-miss arrangement that these station lunchrooms have entered history as "the twenty-minute gulp stop." With a trainload of passengers to serve, the station lunchroom was a busy place, so busy that the service was unbelievably bad and the food was abominable. Only the passenger shot with luck would be able to gulp down some food before his train pulled out. It was necessary to keep one eye on the conductor who, watch in hand, paced impatiently up and down the depot platform. Travelers had to pay before served and sometimes heard the "all aboard" before they could eat. In fact, caterers would bribe conductors to cut the stop short so that food which had been paid for but not eaten could be saved and served again. First-class passengers traveling between Omaha and Sacramento often paid the extra charge so they could ride the weekly Pacific Hotel Express, which did have food on board. By the 1880s, most of the western trains had dining cars.

However, the victims of the vagaries and horrors of depot meals were about to be rescued by another one of those innovative entrepreneurs with which the nineteenth century seemed to abound, Frederick Henry Harvey, a native of London who had emigrated to the United States in 1850. After twenty-six years of running restaurants and working on railroads, Harvey combined the two careers into one when in 1876 he became manager of the depot restaurant at Topeka, Kansas, on the Santa Fe line. For the first time travelers on the line had good, hot food served on clean plates awaiting them at each stop for meals. Harvey even introduced the luxuries of tablecloths and linen napkins. Service, also, was fast. Train conductors helped out matters by wiring ahead the number of customers and by the time the train had panted into the station, hot meals were ready to be served. And Harvey had applied a new and daring solution to the problem of service. He hired waitresses, the famous Harvey Girls, attractive young women of good character, intelligent, and between the ages of 18 and 30. Wearing their crisp white aprons, the Harvey Girls dazzled the western men, who married 5,000 of them.

By the time he died in 1901, Harvey had expanded his operations to include forty-seven depot diners and restaurants in fifteen hotels. He also had taken over the food service on thirty of the Santa Fe's dining cars, including the first, the California Limited. The Santa Fe advertised Harvey's food and service as "the standard of excellence the world over."

Most of the dining cars of the 1880s and 1890s were the last word in luxury and good food, and they caught the imagination of the traveler as nothing else has before or since. Much of the glamour of the era of the steam locomotive centers around this exciting aspect of travel by rail, and the accessories that go with it, from the fascinating menus to the lovely china, glassware, and silver. These form a group of collectibles that are among the most beautiful a railroadiana collector will find.

The menus of the Pullman hotel cars have not been equaled since these cars made their debut in the West with their service on the Northwestern line between Chicago and Omaha. The Christmas, 1890, menu lists twelve courses with forty-five different dishes. Universally, throughout the railroads of that day, the wine steward's lockers were well stocked, and the food excelled that of the best restaurants. First-class passengers ate grand meals in grand style, prepared by Pullman chefs and served by Pullman waiters. Regional dishes often were a part of the menu: fresh trout from streams along the western routes, a variety of game, Georgia peaches, shrimp Creole. Butter served on the Twentieth Century Limited was "made entirely from the cream of purebred Holsteins," and another railroad advertised, "Meals as good as in any New York hotel."

Many railroads were famous for a special food and they featured this in their advertising—the Northern Pacific's Baked Potato Route, for example, or the Great Northern's Route of the Big Red Apple. Sometimes their menus were in the shape of these special foods. The Boston and Maine served Boston baked beans, and the Southern Pacific's salad bowl was so famous, and its recipe so often requested, that it was printed on their menus. Most railroads operated their dining cars at a loss and considered the money well spent, as "riding on the railroad" and "eating on the railroad" caught the imagination of the public.

Collecting menus from this era of the luxurious dining car is a delightful experience for a collector. The American traveler was made to feel like royalty as he looked over a menu that listed broiled pigeon, canvasback duck, potted game, roast beef, cold cuts, quail on toast, sirloin steak, blue-winged teal, a dozen relishes, two dozen desserts, all of them exotic. No wonder he took such a menu home to keep as a souvenir. Those who collect dining car artifacts vicariously experience the Oriental Limited's lounge steward, for instance, serving tea from a silver service at five every afternoon; the music of a Hawaiian string quartet playing in the lounge car during dinner on the Florida Special; the spotless table linen, the vase of cut flowers, the well-appointed table with its shining silver and sparkling glassware; the immaculate, attentive waiters. No wonder so many today also collect the china, glassware, and silver once used on these elegant dining cars.

The Baltimore and Ohio's historical blue china, made for its centennial celebration in 1927, is perhaps the best known and most popular with collectors. A number of china manufacturers were interested in making this blue-and-white dinnerware. One of these was the Buffalo Pottery Company, and several trial pieces made by them have become collector's items. However, the B & O placed the order with the Scammell China Company of Trenton, who made the china for a quarter of a century. The center of each piece portrayed a historical scene along the route of the railroad. Only the larger pieces have the well-known border that shows their motive power down through the years. The border includes a horse-drawn car of 1830; the first American-built locomotive, the Tom Thumb, 1830; the Atlantic of 1832; the Philip E. Thomas, 1838; Winan's Camel-back, 1851; the Mogul 600, 1875; and the Lord Baltimore, 1927. After the diesel came into use, B & O's first diesel-electric engine, No. 51, was worked into the border, and the Lord Baltimore was deleted. This blue china still is being made today, although not by Scammell, and it is being sold at the B & O Museum Gift Shop in Baltimore. The first series is quite rare today, and the second series, featuring the diesel, is rapidly disappearing.

The Missouri Pacific's crack name trains were distinguished for the handsome service plates used on their diners. These have become favorites among collectors. The earlier of the two plates, known as the State Flower pattern, is commonly referred to as the "steam plate" because of the likeness of the line's Sunshine Special steam train in the center. Around the border of the plate are the flowers of the states through which the trains traveled. The coloring is vivid, with black and yellow predominating.

In 1948 this pattern was supplanted by the State Capitols pattern, or "diesel plate," showing the road's new diesel streamliner, The Texas Eagle, in the center, with state capitols around the edge. Medium blue in coloring, this plate was produced until 1961. The double-track scenic location is the same on both plates. While both of these plates are highly collectible today, the diesel is the more difficult to find.

The service plates made by the Buffalo Pottery Company for the Chesapeake and Ohio Railroad were probably among the most striking pieces of dinnerware ever made for any railroad. These were issued in 1932 to celebrate the bicentennial of George Washington's birth, and they featured a reproduction of Gilbert Stuart's *Athenaeum* portrait of Washington, with a rim of gold. A limited number of these were sold to the public on the line's crack train, the George Washington. However, they proved too expensive for general use and were discontinued.

The Buffalo Pottery Company also made dinnerware for the Chesapeake and Ohio for use on The Sportsman. This dinnerware carried the line's corporate symbol, the Chessie Cat, adopted in late 1933, and eventually it became the only pattern used on C & O trains. Another interesting dinner plate was made for the New York, New Haven and Hartford Railroad. The pattern featured an outline map in the center showing the New England states through which the railroad traveled, with the road's streamlined train running across the map. Mountains, a whale, and a clipper ship also are shown on the plate.

Most railroads featured their own exclusive and copyrighted designs on their china with a logo or herald somewhere on each piece. The pieces were designed for durability and stability on a moving train; yet they were colorful and pleasing to the eye. Many roads had a distinctive pattern, which came to be well known and was identified only with their road. One such pattern was the Union Pacific's Harriman Blue, with the railroad's logo and name stamped on the back of each piece. Others featured the region through which the road ran. The Great Northern's Glory of the West pattern sometimes used its famous Rocky Mountain goat and its Mountains and Flowers. The china on the crack Oriental Limited had an appropriately oriental look in coloring and pattern. An interesting children's set used on the Great Northern's diner in the 1920s and 1930s featured colorful character animals with the Rocky Mountain goat logo also displayed on each piece. These must have had a high percentage of breakage—perhaps the reason they are hard to find and very collectible today.

The Pullman Company often used the Indian Tree pattern, purchased from the china company's regular stock, and had the Pullman name added to it. Some railroads simply purchased regular in-stock china patterns and had them backstamped with the railroad's name or initials, along with the hallmark of the manufacturer. The front-marked pieces, however, are the most desired by the collector. Some railroad china was not marked in any way, and these pieces can only be identified by the pattern itself.

Collecting railroad china is relatively new, but it has grown rapidly through the last decade, and not much of it is to be found today. Amtrak has now taken over the railroad dining cars and it provides its own china.

Like china, the dining car silver also is widely collected today. The railroads ordered their silverware from the usual manufacturers of silver-plated ware, among them the International Silver Company, Meriden Britannia Company, Gorham Manufacturing, and Reed and Barton. Most dining car silver was made of 18 percent nickel-silver, silver soldered. Some railroads had patterns made exclusively for them, often for use on their famous name trains. One example is the Chicago, Milwaukee, St. Paul and Pacific's Olympian silverware service. However, many railroads simply used patterns from the manufacturer's regular hotel-restaurant lines and, for this reason, must carry the railroad's identifying marks somewhere on them. Usually the railroad's initials or heralds are engraved on the top side of each piece; they also may be stamped on the bottom, along with the maker's hallmarks. Some have been double-marked, with the railroad's identification on both top and bottom.

Those who remember the delightful experience of dining in the diner may also remember the array of gleaming silverware on each side of the plate. All of this silver is diligently sought after by today's collectors. Besides the various-sized spoons, forks, and knives, there are many other flatware pieces, such as sugar tongs, oyster forks, cheese scoops, or crumb knives. These special pieces often are harder to find because they were not in constant use. Unusually shaped handles or ornamental designs on the handles, such as leaves or shells or fleur-de-lis patterns, have more appeal than the plainer patterns. Pages from old silverware company catalogs show as many as eighteen or twenty pieces of flatware made in each pattern, all available to the railroads and used by them, and thus are available to the diligent collector as well. But to find many or all of these pieces, and to find them all railroad-marked, is quite a challenge.

From the moment the dinner chimes summoned a train's passengers to the paneled mahogany dining car, to the moment the silver finger bowls were set before them, passengers were surrounded with silver serving dishes: menu holders, covered soup tureens, fruit-cocktail bowls, bread trays, butter dishes, gravy boats, coffee servers, sugar and creamers, finger bowls and silver change trays. All serving pieces today demand premium prices. The earlier pieces reflect the Victorian era, and their ornate handles, gooseneck spouts, acorn-type finials, and fleur-de-lis designs make them especially desirable. As with the flatware, all hollow ware also must carry the railroad's identifying marks on them, either on the top or bottom.

No longer do maîtres d' hôtel await the diners in the railroad's elegant dining car. As the railroads practice their economies in all departments, including the few remaining passenger trains with dining cars, the luxuries of yesterday seem far away. Collecting the memorabilia of the dining car era during those golden years helps us to remember them.

When the Prince of Wales traveled from Albany to Boston aboard the Boston and Albany's Special in 1860, he admitted that he was impressed, among other things, by the several saloon cars, which, he noticed, were equipped with shiny brass cuspidors. In those tobacco-chewing years, a spitoon was a necessity, not only on the train, but in every depot, waiting room, and lunch room, and the brass spitoons of these early days are especially collectible. Very few of them are around today, and those that carry the railroad's name or logo are high on the collector's list.

Book matches with the railroad's name or logo—at one time so available they could be picked up freely in every railroad ticket office, restaurant, and depot—now are becoming hard to find. Some of these are very attractive, especially if they date from the years of the name passenger trains, since they usually pictured the fast, limited trains. Those from the steam era are especially desirable. A search through collections of matchbook covers in antique shops or among hobby clubs may unearth covers from railroads no longer in existence. The more recent railroad book matches also are not easy to find, since not many of these have been saved. The stock book or albums of the match collector may contain several of them.

Small, pocket-type cigarette lighters with a railroad's name or logo on them once were widely used and now are being collected. Another challenge is to search for railroad-marked ashtrays. Countless numbers were used in a train's dining, smoking, and parlor cars, and in railroad offices and depots. They were made of glass, ceramic, and metal, in many shapes and sizes, and had the railroad's logo prominently displayed. Smoking items from smoking car lounges, such as the cast-iron floor-model ashtrays, also are being collected. These should carry the railroad's name or insignia.

Note: The souvenir cast-iron matchbox of the Missouri, Kansas and Texas Railroad in the shape of its logo, and the cast-iron, alligator-shaped matchbox of the Monon Route, are now collector's items.

The many souvenir items the railroads put out also offer the collectors a wide variety of objects to look for, since thousands of these were brought out through the years. Those from the earlier years, of course, are more in demand, and many of these have become quite scarce. Souvenirs of later years are more plentiful, and while right now collectors can find any number of these, they are rapidly being picked up. Many souvenirs were handed out freely to the public, or presented to railroad customers, but a lot of them also were sold at railroad depots. There were novelty items of all kinds, such as pocketknives, letter openers, and pocket mirrors, and these are very collectible today. Items representing some advertised feature of a particular road, such as the Northern Pacific's big baked-potato inkwell, or the grizzly-bear paperweight of the Chicago, Milwaukee and St. Paul Railway's Gallatin Gateway to Yellowstone Park, are getting to be real finds. Games and puzzles also were given away as souvenirs, but these are hard to find today in good condition since paper and cardboard items deteriorate through the years.

The Northern Pacific gave away a folding paper fan made in Japan of rice paper and bamboo as a souvenir to promote its tours to the Orient. A variety of paperweights in the form of miniature locomotives was made. A clock in the form of the front end of a locomotive was put out by the Chicago, Milwaukee and St. Paul Railway and featured its Pioneer Limited. A collection of railroad souvenir items never can be considered complete; new items always will be found as the collector continues his search for these interesting reminders of this aspect of the era of steam.

Then there are the baggage checks used universally by anyone riding the rails, past and present. In the early days passengers went into the baggage room themselves and found their own luggage. This proved to be quite a trial for the baggageman. Without proper identification the same piece was often claimed by more than one passenger. The result was that confusion reigned and so did heavy claims against the railroads.

The baggage check was invented by a gentleman named William Morris to resolve the problem. It consisted of two brass checks which were attached to a leather strap. When a passenger checked his trunk or suitcase at the depot baggage room, the baggageman removed the smaller of the two checks from the strap and gave it to him. The larger check was attached to the luggage for transportation to its destination. Upon arrival at the end of the journey, the passenger claimed his belongings by showing the duplicate check. Both the brass checks were then attached to the strap again for use by the next passenger.

Collectors who find these baggage checks and straps today discover that both checks are seldom intact; the smaller duplicate check is usually missing. Probably many of these were never reattached to the strap, perhaps through simple negligence or because they were lost either by the traveler or in the baggage room. Usually baggage checks are found with one check only on the strap, or the check is found without a strap. The brass baggage check eventually was discontinued and replaced by the cardboard claim check used today.

A Christmas Journey

The Lake Shore Michigan Southern Ry.

"Recognized to be the finest in the United States, in point of roadbed, equipment and service."

A Christmas Journey—There are thousands of these delightful railroad ads to be found in the pages of many old magazines, which can be put in your scrapbook or framed as a picture to hang on the wall.

The development of the Pullman sleeping car down through the years is shown in this interesting folder and booklets published years ago. Paper items such as these make historic additions to your paper collection.

The tourists glued many of these railroad travel stickers to their luggage years ago, when traveling by train was the way to go. These old stickers can make a colorful page in your album.

Passengers using this metal step stool to board the Great Northern's Empire Builder, during the steam era, took a step into adventure.

Northern Pacific's breakfast, lunch, and dinner menus, used on their North Coast Limited dining cars in the early 1900s. Many collectors specialize only in dining car menus.

Northern Pacific menu in the shape of a casserole opened to show its contents. The back side pictures their dining car table setting. These unusually shaped menus are very popular with the collector.

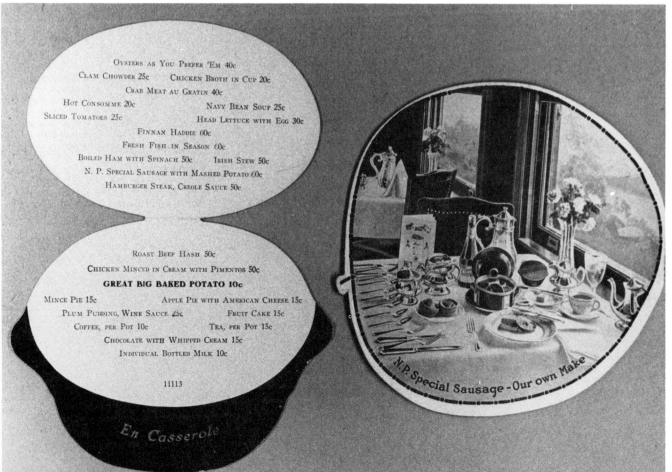

The Baltimore & Ohio's beautiful historical blue centennial china has been a favorite since it was introduced in 1927. Shown here is a dinner plate from an early issue.

The Union Pacific's famous Harriman Blue pattern used in their dining cars long ago.

A cup and saucer from the popular B & O blue china. The cover on the cup kept the coffee from spilling over the edge as the train rounded a curve.

Back side of the Union Pacific's Harriman Blue china shows their well-known Shield logo stamped in blue.

Great Northern trains going west featured a Mountains and Flowers pattern on their dining car china.

The Pullman Company operated dining cars for a few railroads. This piece, in the Indian Tree pattern, was used on their elegant diners years ago.

The Milwaukee road had this pattern in shades of pink over white on the Traveler, one of their name passenger trains.

A glass vinegar cruet, which saw much use on the Great Northern Railway's dining cars during the age of steam. Not many of these have survived.

An elegant cut-glass syrup pitcher, which adorned a Soo Line Railroad dining car table during the Victorian years. A rare piece.

Cocktail set used on the Union Pacific's club cars in the good old days.

A Southern Pacific Railway silver card tray, with an engraving of one of their crack passenger trains across the center. These are really scarce.

Coffee drinkers on the Union Pacific's diners used this coffeepot many years ago. Their famous Salt Lake Route logo is prominently shown on the front of this piece.

During the Victorian years, ornate style coffeepots like this one were the fashion. The Northern Pacific's logo is seen on the front of this piece.

A silver cake stand, which graced the table of a Great Northern Railway's elegant dining car.

Examples of railroad-marked flatware pieces. These have the Great Northern (G.N.) monogram.

A tip was left in this Great
Northern Railway silver change
tray for the good food and service.

A bread tray from a Soo Line dining car,
showing their early banner logo. Most collectors prefer top-marked pieces over bottom-
marked pieces.

Vendors sold milk to the passengers in the coach cars to drink with their sandwiches. This bottle is from the Northern Pacific Railway.

There were many book matches and ashtrays distributed by the railroads down through the years. Here are some examples.

Some of the many cigarette lighters, which also were handed out by the railroads back in those days.

A rare item is this Monon Route bronze matchholder in the shape of an alligator. The alligator's back is the hinged cover.

Another collector's item is this cast-iron matchbox in the shape of the Missouri, Kansas & Texas Railway's logo. Names of railroad officials are impressed on the back side.

A metal grizzly bear souvenir paperweight, put out years ago by the Chicago, Milwaukee and St. Paul Railway to promote their Gallatin Gateway to Yellowstone Park.

The famous Northern Pacific's big baked potato featured in their diners was made in an inkwell shape many years ago as a souvenir advertising piece. The top opens up and the inkwell is at the bottom. A choice collector's item today.

Front and back of a rice paper and bamboo folding souvenir fan, made in Japan for the Northern Pacific Railway to promote their tours to the Orient around the turn of the century.

Souvenir pocket mirror issued by the Frisco Lines many years ago.

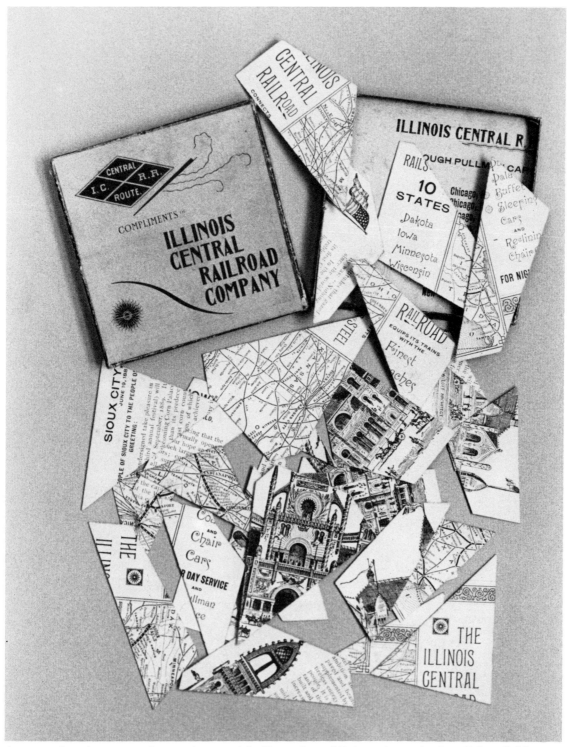

A rare cardboard jigsaw puzzle, compliments of the Illinois Central Railway during the Corn Palace Celebration, June 19, 1889, at Sioux City, Iowa.

An old souvenir clock from the Chicago, Milwaukee & St. Paul Railway to promote their Pioneer Limited when it first went into service.

The Chicago Great Western Railway put out a souvenir paperweight featuring their colorful maple leaf emblem, used around the turn of the century.

Many paperweights were made years ago in the form of miniature locomotives. These are highly collectible.

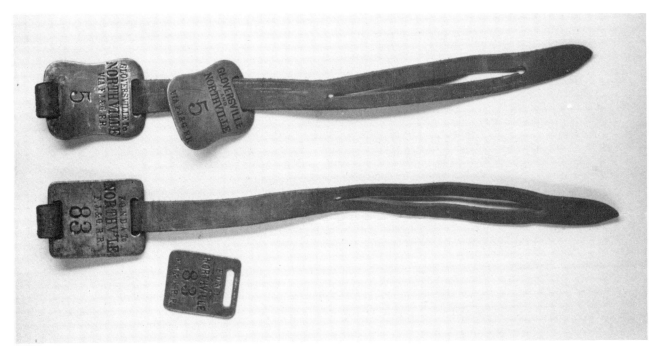

A pair of these old brass baggage checks on their leather straps. One was removed from the strap and given to the passenger, who used it to claim his baggage. Occasionally the loose check was lost.

Back in the early days these brass checks were used on the traveler's baggage to avoid confusion in the baggage room.

6 I've Been Working on the Railroad

THE INSIDE MEN

Builder's Locomotive Plates • Caps and Breast Badges • Uniform Buttons • Engineer Caps • Pocket Watches • Watch Fobs • Depot Clocks • Lanterns • Ticket Punches

From the day Horatio Allen first put his hand upon the throttle of the Stourbridge Lion—August 8, 1829—the engineer was thought of as the man who "ran the train." Down through the years no occupation has so captured the imagination of the American boy as that of the locomotive engineer, and the thought may never have crossed his mind that anyone other than the engineer was the "boss" of the train. After all, he was king, seated on his throne on the right side of the cab, a hero, and given the choice, many a boy would rather climb the cab and run the train than be president of the United States.

Once engineers also considered themselves "masters of the train," but a permanent shift in responsibility came about in 1842 when Abe Hammil was engineer on the New York and Erie Railroad. At this time, there was no way for the conductor to signal the engineer that he wanted the train to stop, other than for him to climb the roof of the cars and shout or throw something to catch the engineer's attention. Ebenezer Ayres, a new conductor on the New York and Erie line, was moved by the inconvenience to give this some thought. He rigged up a rope over the top of the cars and tied a stick to the end next to the engine. He told Hammil to stop the train when the stick began to bob up and down. But Hammil had his own ideas as to who gave orders and for what. As soon as the train was under way, he cut down the piece of wood. All Ayres pulled was a slack piece of rope. It happened again on the next trip. That settled it for Ayres. When the train stopped at the end of the run, he took off his coat, headed for the cab, knocked Hammil to the ground, and pounded him until Hammil agreed that Ayres was the boss of the train and gave the orders. From then on, the conductor always has had absolute authority over the train—proving, once again, that all decisions are not made in the head office.

In this chapter we will be describing the great variety of collectibles that have come down to us from those colorful men, and sometimes women, who worked on the railroad—the "inside men" (conductors, brakemen, porters) who were and are familiar to the traveling public and the "outside men" (engineers, firemen, switchmen) who make the trains go. Their uniform buttons and cap badges, their locks and keys, and their lanterns are just a few of the many collectibles associated with those who spent their lives working on the railroad.

Perhaps as a carry-over from steamship days, the conductor first was known as the "captain" of the train. He runs it, gives the orders, and the engineer does not even take the train out of the station without the conductor's highball.

In the early days trainmen did not wear uniforms. The conductor, instead, usually wore a broadcloth cutaway coat with brass buttons and a gold watch and chain proudly and prominently displayed. He wore a tall top hat with a narrow metal strip with the word *Conductor* in front. This was held in place by an elastic, and was the forerunner of the cap and breast badges, which are so collectible today. In spite of his identification, he sometimes had trouble collecting the fares. One conductor got into a fistfight with a suspicious western senator who was unwilling to surrender his ticket until he was sure it was to the right person. Not too long after that, train employees were required to wear uniforms.

The conductor's lot was a varied one. With his lantern—often bearing his name—the conductor had to make rounds at night through dimly lighted cars. Then there was the matter of Bible reading. When trains began to run on Sunday, Vermont passed a law requiring that the Captain of the Train read the Bible to his passengers every Sunday, and an ornate wrought-iron shelf was put up in each car to hold the Bible. These Bibles, as well as the shelves on which they sat, are collector's items today.

No drinking water was available on the early trains. The conductor would carry a small kettle with a glass on either side of the spout and he would sell drinking water to the passengers—doing a rushing business on a hot day. Drinking water finally was made available in a tank at one end of the coach with a tin drinking cup attached to it by a chain. All passengers drank from the same cup. Not until much later did the paper cup come into use.

While conductors may have been "elected" on some railroads, the route to becoming Captain of the Train usually was long and hard, with all aspects of railroading to be learned along the way.

In the 1830s the engineer did not ride in a cab. He stood on an open platform in winter and summer, taking the weather as it came. It was 1842 before a few roads added a canopy to their cabs. By 1850 an all-wood cab was in general use, and, by the 1860s and 1870s, these often were ornately lettered, some with fancy gold-leaf scrolls. All-metal cabs did not come into general use until the 1890s. Perhaps the covered cab was a result of early backseat driving. In 1838, large glass tubes of water were attached at the fire end of the locomotive boilers, so the engineer could watch the water level. These also were in plain sight of the passengers, who kept their eyes glued on them, letting the engineer know if the water was getting low.

Many of the early roads were single-track roads, necessitating a sidetrack at places along the line to hold one train while the other passed. Midway post markers were set up along the tracks to show the turnouts, and the locomotive that cleared a midway mark first had the right-of-way. Sometimes, though, both trains would reach the midway mark at the same time, and the right-of-way then might be settled only after a free-for-all, involving not only the engineer, but the rest of the crew and even some of the passengers. The engineer of the losing train simply had to back his train to the last turnout, no matter how far away.

When trains began to run at night, lights were needed. Horatio Allen devised the first headlight by attaching two small flatcars to the front of the engine. He covered the floor of the car with a deep layer of sand and on it he kept a wood fire burning in a makeshift pot. This must have beeen quite a sight in the middle of the night.

Later, large candles in glass cases were used as headlights. By the 1850s a box-shaped headlight of sheet metal containing a whale-oil lamp fitted with reflectors was in fairly general use. A locomotive usually was assigned to its own engineer and he would often furnish his own headlight, embellishing it to his own taste and even taking it home at night. The headlight was mounted on an ornate metal bracket, and often it was decorated with landscape paintings, or even portraits. These are museum pieces today. The engineer took great pride in his engine and usually maintained a strict "hands-off" policy, regarding it as his personal property. He was not willing to let anyone else run it; he knew "her" and "she" knew him, and they worked together as a team.

Engineer and conductor have both been vital to the train's operation since the day in 1829 when the Master of Transportation, John T. Clarke, collected the tickets from the passengers, mounted the tender attached to the engine, and blew a blast on his small tin horn to signal engineer Dan Mathews to start the De Witt Clinton on its memorable run. But it has been the engineer, in his striped cap and red bandanna, silhouetted at the cab window, who has captured the imagination of young and old. The seat on the left-hand side of the cab belonged to the fireman—but his many duties did not often given him a chance to sit on it. He, like the engineer, braved the summer heat and rain and winter snow and cold, in those early precab days. On runs he did little else besides toss cordwood to the hungry engine, or help load the tender at wood stops along the route. The fireman paid farmers and other men who hauled the wood to the fuel stops, and he used special tokens issued by the railroads for this purpose. These were redeemable at the railroads' offices, and they are highly prized as collectibles today.

Whether the use of coal in later years made his job easier is a good question. Besides needing a strong back, a fireman also needed a certain degree of skill in tossing it evenly through the fire door and into the firebox. To keep the fire hot enough to suit the engineer, he shoveled many tons of the fossil fuel before the oil burner and the stoker appeared on the scene. And the fireman's scoop now has taken its place on the list of collectibles. The fireman also was the man who crawled out of the cab onto the locomotive's running board as the train coasted downgrade, and edged precariously along the side of the hot boiler to fill the cylinder cups with hot tallow. This feat earned him his nickname of "tallowpot." However, nothing was too dangerous, and no work was too hard as long as he kept his eye on the cab's right-hand seat. Someday, in the orderly fashion of railroad promotions, that seat would be his.

About 1840 locomotive bells became standard equipment on engines, but their main function was to warn both humans and animals to watch out for the coming train. In the very early days, a man on horseback rode ahead of the locomotive waving a flag and shouting, "The train is coming." When a bell was added, it was the fireman's job to ring it, and many a fireman would develop such a distinctive touch on the bell that his friends and family would become familiar with its tone and cadence. When President Lincoln's body was carried by train from Chicago to Springfield in 1865, the engine's muffled bell tolled the entire distance. Many a bell has outlasted the Iron Horse on which it was mounted, and they are widely collected today.

In those early days one of the many duties of the brakeman on a passenger train was to fill the woodboxes at the end of each car, and to keep up the fires in the hungry stoves. He carried the key to the woodbox with him, so that chilly passengers could not throw extra chunks of wood in the stove when he was elsewhere. In addition to tending the fires, the brakeman was the man who strung the bell cord across the cars, kept signal lamps and lanterns cleaned and filled (including the conductor's), hauled the baggage from the station to the cars, twisted the brake wheels at the ends of the cars when the train was ready to stop, and helped the conductor with the tickets when the coaches were packed. In between runs he helped to assemble the train and to clean it. In comparison to his counterpart on the freight train, however, his job was a cinch. The freight brakeman had to climb the roof and run the catwalk from car to car to set the brakes by hand in all kinds of weather. He was in real danger of skidding on ice-covered car roofs in the winter, and of losing his life if he lost his footing and fell.

From the beginning, how to fasten the cars together was a problem. Crude fastenings were devised at first—hooks, chains, bars, all were tried. A link-and-pin type of coupling became the most common, and it was referred to as the Lincoln pin. These old Lincoln pins are displayed in railroad museums today. Before Eli Janney invented the automatic coupler and George Westinghouse the air brake, many thousands of brakemen lost fingers and even hands, or were crushed to death between the cars while attempting to insert the pin into the link. It was not until 1893, however, that President Benjamin Harrison signed the Railroad Safety Appliance Act, requiring all cars to be equipped with air brakes and automatic couplers.

Down through the years, yard switchmen equipped with three-foot-long hickory brake clubs, applied leverage to the hand-operated brake wheels in order to stop the cars. Today it is a matter of simply pushing buttons in the control tower. Even the "gandy dancer," the track worker who got his name from his jiglike movements as he tamped the ties, is being replaced by machines, which now do the backbreaking work of keeping the tracks in repair.

But as the tracks continued to be laid and trains to travel over them, the need arose for stations where passengers could buy tickets and wait for the train. In some instances, houses were used as stations; sometimes a ticket booth was all that the railroad provided.

When the small depot did come into being, a station agent was assigned to it. In the early days he was known as the Master of the Depot, and his duties consisted of doing everything: selling tickets, handling baggage, keeping the stove burning, sweeping the floor. One eastern railroad, in its "Instructions for Conductors and Engineers," gave the Master of the Depot these instructions: "If at any time a train should not arrive at either depot, (a distance of 12 miles apart), you shall start immediately on horseback to learn the cause of the delay."

Eventually the depot became a town's social center, with train time the big event of the day, "Meet me at the depot" a favorite meeting place. Old postcards with depots on them are now being collected.

In a small depot, the telegrapher's job went hand in hand with that of station agent, and today his key and sounder are highly collectible. Another of the station agent's duties was to set the order board for each train, and dispatch the train orders, using his hoop (another collectible). These were snatched by the crew as the train thundered past the station, and it called for dexterity on both the giving and receiving ends.

The sound of the locomotive whistle has become engrained in the American consciousness down through the years. No boy was prouder of his new toy than an engineer was of his locomotive's whistle, and he devised all kinds of gadgetry to give it a tone so distinctive that it would be recognized as his special whistle. A classic example is the ballad of Casey Jones, the Brave Engineer: "The switchmen knew by the engine's moans—that the man at the throttle was Casey Jones."

For generations Americans had lived with the sound of the locomotive's whistle, whether they were in the backwoods country or in the big city. It left a deep impression on people of all walks of life and those who heard it have not forgotten it. The whistle talked to them; sometimes it called up visions of a faraway teeming metropolis; sometimes it brought a lonesome feeling of being far from home. A lot of romance is associated with these vanished steam whistles, and to own one is a fine addition to any collection. Recordings have preserved their sound, and the records are available at record shops.

There have been more than 100 builders of steam locomotives in this country down through the years. Most of these locomotives were identified with a builder's plate, which came in a variety of shapes and sizes. Many of the classic locomotives of the 1860s and 1870s had a large, ornate, monogram-style plate mounted between the huge driving wheels. In later years these were made of solid cast metal. They are known today as "locomotive builder's plates." They carried the name of the builder and the location of the shops, the date the engine was built, and a serial number. The plate was affixed to the locomotive, usually to the smokebox. Some builders used a distinctively shaped plate, such as the Baldwin Locomotive Works' large circle or the diamond used by the Lima Locomotive Works. Others had a small rectangular plate or a circular disk, and these are the types most readily available to collectors today. Of course, plates bearing an early date, ornate in design, or of an unusual shape or size are the rarities, and these are not easy to find.

In the early days, when trainmen did not wear a regulation cap or uniform, so many problems arose that they began to affix an identification badge of some sort to their regular hats or coats. Before long, however, all employees—passenger conductor, brakeman, station agent, baggageman, porter, police officer, down to the waiter-coach attendant and cook—came under the Rules and Specifications Governing the Uniforming of Employees, which stated that "employees on duty must wear the prescribed badge and uniform, and be neat in appearance." Badges were furnished by the railroad, and if an employee left the train's service, he was required to return his badge.

The cap badge came in a number of styles, from a plain panel to those which were quite ornate. The lettering or numbering was stamped on some badges and filled in with black enamel against a polished background; others had embossed titles or lettering against a gold- or nickel-plated background. The more ornate styles had brightly polished raised letters and numbers against a contrasting colored background. Most badges included the name of the railroad on them. Breast badges also were furnished, as were silk cap bands which fitted around the cap and had the occupation embroidered in gold or silver letters.

The collecting of these cap and breast badges in their many variations is growing rapidly. Their value depends upon the badge's condition, shape, style, and ornateness. Those for unusual or unique occupations are the most difficult to find; conductor or brakeman badges are the most common. Caps were always in uniform, regular styles, and in navy or black.

Uniforms had regulation buttons and carried on them either the name of the railroad, its initials, or the occupation designation, such as porter, agent, conductor. All of these buttons are collectible. A railroad would purchase its buttons from button manufacturers. Made with a gold or silver finish, they were either dome-shaped or had a flat face. They usually came in two sizes, the large size for the coat and the smaller size for sleeves and vest, but exceptions can be found. Buttons with the name of an early railroad or with an unusual occupation are the ones most collectors search for. The coat lapel emblems and pins worn by railroad employees are also very collectible.

The engineer's cap was the product of a fireman's ingenuity back in 1905. One windy day, when the bandanna an engineer had wrapped around his head for protection blew off and sailed off down the track, he decided that perhaps a piece of cloth could be fashioned into a cap with a visor. He mentioned it to his wife, who bought some heavy material and made a cap he wore to work the next day. She had sewn a sweatband into the cap, and had made it big enough to pull down over the ears. It was virtually windproof, and it was a hit. All of his co-workers wanted one, and his wife was kept busy making them. Soon this ingenious cap, or one like it, had become standard headgear for engineers.

An interesting Wisconsin Central Railroad timetable for 1900 shows an "usher" in uniform at the Wisconsin Central Station in Chicago. He is wearing a bright red cap with *Usher* on it. The timetable reads: "Patrons of the Wisconsin Central Railway in passing through Chicago may require some assistance in the way of having their hand baggage taken from or to train and carriage or bus, or in many other ways, and they will find all that is desired in this respect in the service of the Ushers at the Central Passenger Station, who are uniformed with brown suit and red cap. They will be waiting at all trains prepared to assist passengers, and it is hoped that our patrons will fully avail themselves of this additional provision for their comfort." This perhaps is where the term *redcap* originated.

The railroads' most precious asset was time, and accurate time was an absolute necessity, down to the very second. Every train must arrive and depart on an accurate time schedule, and, furthermore, safety dictated that trains move, meet, and pass on schedule. Time was so crucial and uniformity of time schedules so important that in 1883, Standard Time, the concept of dividing the country into time zones, was adopted throughout the United States, a measure sponsored by the railroads.

The railroads required that conductor and engineer compare their watches before starting their run, and this was a familiar sight before the train left the station, going back to the early days. The rest of the crew compared their watches with either the conductor or the engineer to be sure all watches agreed. Each man took personal pride in owning a reliable watch; it was his constant companion. There are many watches that were carried in the pockets of men who worked on the railroad, but these old timepieces cannot be considered "authentic" railroad watches, in the same category as the family heirloom, inherited from Uncle John, conductor of the Overland Express.

Timepieces used by train dispatchers, conductors, enginemen, brakemen, yardmasters, and yard engine foremen had to be compared with a master clock before each day's work could begin. These clocks, corrected daily to conform with the official time signals telegraphed throughout the country by the United States Naval Observatory, were essential for keeping the trains running on time.

Railroad men had to turn in their watches for checking at regular intervals, and the watch inspector would compare them with a master clock to see if they were keeping perfect time. The inspector was not allowed to pass any watch that was not up to standard. A railroad watch usually was open face; it had large black numerals for easy reading at all times, generally 16 size, with not less than 17 and up to 21 jewels, and with adjustment to five positions and for temperature as well.

A trainman's watch, at one time or another in its daily use, could be in any one of these five positions: dial up, or flat on its back; back up, or flat on its face; stem up, or in the position a watch naturally takes in the pocket; 3:00 o'clock up, or as the watch might be if it slipped over to the left in the pocket; 9:00 o'clock up, or as it would be if the watch slipped over to the right in the pocket. Originally, the watch did not have to be adjusted to position but, as time passed, railroad inspectors were not allowed to pass any watches not adjusted to these five positions. As railroad requirements kept growing tighter, the sixth adjustment position—12:00 o'clock down when the stem is in an upside-down position—was added. This was a superior timepiece and it was accepted by railroads anywhere in the world.

Ball pocket watches have played a major role in keeping the railroads running on time, and they are known almost everywhere as the Official Railroad Standard watch. The approval for these standards came from a man named Webb C. Ball who, during the 1890s, instituted a system of inspection and servicing of railroad watches by reliable jewelers to guarantee accurate performance. Ball did not manufacture his own watches, but had various watch factories, such as Hamilton, Elgin, Waltham, to name a few, make them to his specifications. Then they were tested at his plant in Cleveland, Ohio. The Official Railroad Standard was the trademark on the dial, and these were found in the pockets of many railroad men.

The railroads made Americans the greatest watchmakers in the world, producing some of the finest railroad watches money could buy. Another favorite pocket watch among railroad men was the Hamilton, backed by the slogans "The Watch of Railroad Accuracy" and "The Railroad Timekeeper of America." When Hamilton first began to manufacture pocket watches, almost their entire production was purchased by railroad men. The Illinois Watch Company's Bunn Special, Waltham's Vanguard, and Elgin's Veritas also were widely used by railroad men.

Many watch manufacturers during the heyday of railroading attempted to board the bandwagon by selling watches to railroad men. They would give their watches special eye-catching railroad names, such as Trainmen's Special or Railway Special. Others would have an engraved design of a train on the case, or a gold inlaid locomotive on the back side of a silver case, or they would show a locomotive on the movement. The unsuspecting watch collector today can be taken in easily by these substandard timepieces. Collectors should instead seek out the many watches that can be indentified definitely as "approved railroad watches."

A mention should be made here of the railroad depot clock. While the trainmen's watch was not usually seen by the public, depot clocks were the timekeepers the people always saw. They hung on the depot wall, and they kept the train on time, as far as the public was concerned, ticking away as the passengers watched the hour hand for the arrival or departure of the train, confident in its accuracy. It was the duty of the station agent to keep the depot clocks wound and set at the correct time. These key-wind clocks eventually were replaced by electric models. These old depot clocks are much in demand today. Most of them do not carry a railroad name, but when they do, the clock is that much more desirable.

The trainman's watch generally was worn on a gold chain across the vest, or on a leather strap hanging from the small watch pocket. A Brotherhood fob or medal or a railroad emblem also would dangle from the watch chain or the strap. These overlooked treasures from the pocket watch era also are now beginning to be recognized by the watch collector.

There is the story of Richard W. Sears who embarked on his road to riches in 1883 when he was a nineteen-year-old station agent and telegraph operator for the Minneapolis and St. Louis Railway at North Redwood, Minnesota. A shipment of watches arrived at the depot, unconsigned. Nobody claimed them. In those days it was common practice for distributors to ship goods to small railroad depots in the hopes that someone would buy the shipment for resale. Sears decided to take the shipment. He contacted other agents along the line, offering them watches for resale. He paid twelve dollars apiece and sold them for fourteen dollars each. The agents would resell them for sixteen dollars, and each made a two-dollar profit. Sears sold all the watches and promptly ordered more. By 1886 his business of selling watches to railroad employees was so good that he left the railroad and started the R. W. Sears Watch Company. As business increased, he hired a watchmaker, A. C. Roebuck, as a partner—the forerunner of Sears, Roebuck today.

The development of the railroad lantern has had an interesting history, involving numerous patents to improve this seemingly simple birdcage down through the years. The lantern has played an important role in railroading. It was necessary for signaling at night, and no railroadman was without his lantern at his side. From the conductor on down, it was part of his equipment.

There were times when it was even used by the "revenue" passengers, as this notice tacked to the wall of a small town depot many years ago tells us:

Notice to Passengers

Train No. 7 westbound is due here at 1014 PM daily

Train No. 8 eastbound is due here at 611 AM daily

There is no railroad employee on duty at this station at that time so that it will be necessary for revenue passengers to use the necessary signals to stop these trains if they wish to board them.

In daylight use the white flag.

At night use the white globed lantern.

To light the lantern raise the globe so that you can more easily light the wick. When wick has been lit replace the globe and also push the top of the lantern down so it snaps into place so that it will not blow out when you take it outside.

To stop the train use the lantern or flag as the case may be and stand on the station platform facing the train when it shows up and swing the lantern or flag back and forth about knee high until the engineer answers your signal by two short whistles.

Then if the time permits extinguish the lantern and set it inside waiting room door.

These trains stop on flag for revenue passengers only.

Matches have been left near the lantern.

Then there was the large accumulation of lanterns that could be seen daily on an Illinois railway station platform in the 1870s. This was confusing to the passersby and when someone asked why all the lanterns, they were told that they were for revenue passengers who took the early morning train to Chicago. They had to walk through a heavily wooded area in the dark to reach the station and they used the lanterns to light their way. They left the lanterns at the depot and used them again at night when they walked home.

Lanterns have played a romantic role in preventing many train disasters. There is the legend of Kate Shelley who lived on a small farm in Iowa near the Chicago and Northwestern main line where it crossed a trestle over Honey Creek. Further on the track crossed the Des Moines River over a long wooden bridge.

On the night of July 6, 1881, there was a violent rainstorm. As Kate listened to the storm, she also heard a pilot locomotive on the trestle over the creek. The pilot was testing the bridge for safety because the creek was swollen with the rising water and the Fast Atlantic Express train was due to arrive at any minute. Suddenly Kate heard the pilot engine crash through the weakened trestle. She was only fifteen years old but she realized that she must reach the men in the wrecked pilot, and she also must try to stop the Fast Express before it reached the broken trestle. She lighted a lantern and started out in the storm. When she reached the scene, she saw by the light of the lantern that two of the engine crew were desperately hanging on to trees at the creek's edge. Frantic, she pressed on to the Des Moines River bridge and started to cross to reach help at the station on the other side. Halfway across the bridge, the wind blew out her lantern, leaving her in darkness. She crawled across the ties in the dark, with the river raging below. At last she stumbled into the station. The station agent took his lantern and flagged down the Express just in time.

This brave act made Kate Shelley a heroine, and she has been honored by railroadmen down through the years in the many stories, songs, and poems that have been dedicated to her. One of them ends:

> Let others sing of heroes,
> Such praise is due, I guess.
> But I extol Kate Shelley,
> Who saved the Fast Express.

Competition was keen among manufacturers of lanterns and headlights. The Star Headlight and Lantern Company, with a thirty-year record, advertised in 1915 that "our devices, arising out of the ashes of the past, and without fear of prejudice, stand unexcelled before the eyes of the railroad public, and their value and usefulness are attested by their many users." Their slogan: "We Light the Way."

The conductor's lantern was a fancy cut above the signalman's; it was of polished brass, or nickel-plated over brass, often with a two-colored globe. The conductor's name sometimes was etched on it, usually within a wreath.

The signalman's lantern, on the other hand, was more utilitarian. It had to be strong and durable, made for rugged use, designed to meet all of his many requirements—the handle always in position for easy grasping, and the flame adjustable without removing the oil font or globe. There could be no loose ends to catch his clothing, and the wick had to remain lighted in violent windstorms or when on top of a fast-moving train. No complicated mechanism could hinder him in his signaling for, as the old railroad saying went, "Many a railroadman's life has gone out when his lantern light went out."

There were many lantern manufacturers, and the lantern collector should make a study of the various types that were made throughout the years, as there are special features that should be carefully noted. In this category are switch stand lamps, car inspector's lamps, trackwalker lamps, caboose marker lamps, engine classification lamps, and a miscellany of other railroad lamps, all of which also are very collectible today.

After the conductor highballed the engineer and the train began to roll, the conductor, with ticket punch in hand, began to collect and punch the passenger's tickets. Making his way through the train, he would enter each coach and call out, "Tickets, please." Ordinarily it would take him from five to twenty minutes to punch and collect them, depending upon the number of passengers in a coach. This was known in railroad language as "lifting transportation."

Credit for the ticket punch is given to the early conductors of the Erie Railway, who were the first to invent it. Before this, the conductor would cancel the ticket by simply marking it with a pencil, but this did not prove satisfactory. The ticket punch came into common use on all railroads and it still is being used today, since no better system has been devised.

Each conductor had his own ticket punch, with a particular size and shaped design in the die. Some railroads have used hundreds of different designs, which were made specifically for their punches. The Missouri Pacific has used more than 1,500 shaped designs down through the years, and the Pennsylvania Railroad well over 2,500. New punches were issued to replace those lost or worn out.

The individual design of each conductor's punch was as good as his signature, and it was so distinctive that the Auditor of Passenger Receipts on any railroad could quickly identify the conductor who punched the ticket. He simply matched the design in the ticket hole with a record book of ticket punch designs for every conductor in the railroad's employ. If a conductor forgot to sign his trip report, the tickets accompanying that report would easily identify the conductor by the type of hole punched in the ticket. Occasionally a conductor would also use his nickel-plated pliers to punch his design after his signature as a quick identification against forgery.

Conductor ticket punches came in many different shapes and styles and they make an interesting collection. The countless number of old railroad tickets found with these individual punch marks on them is fascinating to see. They could tell many an interesting story.

THE OUTSIDE MEN

Telegrapher's Keys and Sounders • Wire Insulators • Wax Sealers • Switch Locks and Keys • Oil, Kerosene and Water Cans • Torches • Sledgehammers and Other Tools • Date Nails • Commemorative Medals

Perhaps the most important railroad telegraph message ever sent was that from Promontory, Utah, on May 10, 1869. At 12:45 a telegrapher tapped out the message *D O N E*—four letters in Morse code that signaled to cities across the country that the rails had been joined. Bells were rung so that the townspeople would know that the last spike had been driven linking the East and the West. This was the first nationwide telegraphic hookup in history.

Before the telegraph came into being, trains were operated by working timetables authorizing the movement of the trains. The result was innumerable delays as trains waited for each other. The telegraph did more than anything else to speed up railroad operations. However, the enormous effect the invention of the telegraph had on the railroad was not recognized until 1851, although Morse had invented the telegraph in 1844.

A Mr. Minot, superintendent of the Erie Railway, was sitting in a westbound train on a siding, impatiently awaiting an overdue eastbound train when he thought of telegraphing the next station to ask if the eastbound train had passed. He learned it had not. He then sent the first train order ever to go by telegraph: "Hold Eastbound Train till Further Orders." Minot gave the conductor of his train instructions to proceed, but the engineer refused to follow the conductor's orders. Minot took the throttle himself and ran the train to the next station. Still no eastbound train. Again he telegraphed west to the next station. Again no train. This continued until he arrived at the station where he met the other train, hours earlier than if they had remained on the siding, adhering to the timetable rule, and waiting for the eastbound train.

The Erie Railroad quickly adopted the telegraph to move its trains, and other lines soon followed. Thus began the railroad's system of running on train orders telegraphed from station to station. The railroads soon employed telegraph operators in large numbers, and telegraph instruments became a vital part of every railroad's operation.

Many exciting tales have been woven around the railroad telegrapher, and it is a known fact that some railroad presidents began their careers as "brass pounders" in small-town depots. The clicking sounds of the telegraph instruments attracted the attention of many a lad, and wondering what the messages were all about and where they were going often stirred their imaginations and prompted them to learn the Morse code so that someday they, too, might become railroad telegraph operators. Station operators pounded out many exciting messages in their day, and railroad books and magazines are filled with Morse code stories. There were women operators, too, on the dot-and-dash circuit, and they were highly skilled.

The key and sounder are vanishing from the scene, now that telephone, radio, and CTC (Centralized Traffic Control) are dispatching the messages. Many small-town stations have been closed and the operators have gone on to other jobs. But railroad telegraph equipment has now become popular with collectors of railroadiana. The two most popular items are the key and sounder, especially those that have the name of the railroad and the manufacturer on them. The patent date is also desirable. The sounder is usually of brass, as is the key, which has a Bakelite disk.

Insulators, used to insulate the singing wires on a line of poles along the railroad track from one station to another, are a part of this category, and the collecting of these has grown rapidly in the last decade. Ever since the invention of the telegraph, insulators have been made of both glass and pottery, and various glass companies manufactured them by the thousands. Clear glass and glass in various shades of green are the most common, but they also were made in cobalt blue, amber, amethyst, carnival, and other colors. Most of them are marked with the manufacturer's name, and many have the patent date on them. The earliest insulators are, of course, the most difficult to find. Those that have the name of the railroad marked on them are especially preferred.

Note: Don't overlook the familiar scissor phone and other types of telephones that were so much a part of the station operators' equipment.

The railroads initiated the use of wax sealers early in their history. Envelopes and packages containing valuable goods, important papers, tickets, currency, etc., had wax seals affixed to the flaps to safeguard their contents. The use of these wax seals by the railroads has an interesting history:

Losses kept plaguing the railroads, with the mysterious disappearance of valuables and currency. When they were opened at their destination, envelopes containing money often contained worthless paper instead of the currency, which had vanished. Examination of the envelope indicated that the flaps apparently had been steamed open and then reglued. A way to stop the pilferage had to be found. Wax seals had been used in ancient times, in Europe and during the colonial years in America to safeguard documents and confidential messages.

The railroads decided to use this method of guarding against tampering. It was an immediate success, and was quickly recognized as an effective deterrent. The wax seals would be affixed to the envelope generally in three places along the gummed edge of the flap. In some instances, a double envelope was used; or one box was placed inside another and wax seals applied to both. The station agent would sign and bear witness to the fact that the seals were intact. The unbroken seals assured the receiver that there had been no tampering or pilfering along the railroad route, either at the point of origin or its terminus. Inevitably, in some instances, losses did occur through a number of ingenious tricks used by professional thieves, but eventually their methods were detected and circumvented.

The railroads and express companies used wax sealers until after World War II, when the practice was discontinued. With the ending of the era of wax sealers, many of the sealers ended up in station agents' desk drawers or were relegated to the wastebasket.

They still can be found today, however. They may have a fancy or a plain wooden handle, and usually are about four inches tall, with a round or oval brass or bronze head (matrix) varying in thickness. The earlier ornate wood handles were often hand fashioned. Others were a one-piece tool about three inches tall, all brass or bronze, with a toadstool- or bulb-type handle and a round or oval matrix. The matrix carries the name of the railroad, town, and state, or route number. Letters are engraved or stamped in the matrix in reverse, and when the matrix is pressed into a pool of hot melted sealing wax, a legible embossed impression is the result. The matrix sometimes bore a special designation, such as freight office, freight agent, ticket office, dining car, commissary, passenger station, or paymaster.

Some collectors specialize in wax sealers from a certain state—perhaps the state they live in—and they collect sealers from that state only, such as, "A.T. & S.F. RR, Agent, Lyons, Kansas." I have a collection of Chicago, Milwaukee and St. Paul Railway Division sealers. One example: "C.M. & St.P. Ry, Oacoma, S.D., I & D Division" (Iowa and Dacotah Division). Among the rarities in wax sealers are those few which include the name of the railroad as well as the name of an express company that served the same line. Example: "Am. Ry. Exp. Co., C. & N.W. Ry., Merrill, Iowa." Another rarity is a sealer with a territorial marking, such as "A.T. & S.F. Ry, Agent, Bartlesville, I.T." (Indian Territory).

Again, you may encounter a sealer, as I did, with the name of a town that appears to be nonexistent and, if you are persevering, you will try to locate that town. I found a sealer with this impression: "C.M. & St.P. Ry, Des M. Div.-Manthorps." Unable to find the town of Manthorps listed in any of my Official Railway Guides, old timetables, or old railroad maps, I contacted the home office of the railroad company, the historical society of that state, plus many old-time railroad agents on that division, to try to learn something about the town and its location. No one could help me, and it still remains a mystery.

There also are express company sealers that are similar to those used by the railroads with the same make and style. They either have a wood handle with a bronze matrix, or are all one piece in bronze or brass. Some of these: Wells Fargo Express, Adams Express, American Express, National Express, United States Express, and Railway Express Agency. Many collectors specialize in express company sealers.

Look for some of the accessories that go with the wax sealers, such as the small spirit torches used by agents to melt the wax, the sticks of sealing wax, and the old railroad and express money package envelopes bearing the original wax seal impressions. Collecting these wax sealers is a fascinating and often overlooked category of railroadiana.

Interest in the collecting of railroad locks and keys dates from the early days of railroading and, as a result, they always have been near the top of the list of railroadiana collectibles. Thousands of them were made of brass, bronze, or iron, and they were used widely for switches, signals, depots, cabooses, coaches, tool sheds, and so on.

Of all these locks and keys, the switch lock and the switch key are most in demand among collectors, and particularly the early all-bronze heart-shaped switch lock and its key. The switches were kept locked at all times, and the switchman guarded his key carefully so it would not fall into unauthorized hands. This was especially true in wartime to prevent sabotage. A familiar sight used to be the switchman using his key to unlock the lock at the switch stand and bending the rail to open the gate so a rolling string of varnish could pass on to the main line.

Years ago I found my first railroad switch key in a box of miscellaneous old keys. I set out immediately to try to find the same railroad markings on a switch lock that the key would open. Luck was with me—not long afterward I came across the lock. This started me on collecting switch locks and keys. However, the rest was not so easy.

In my continuous search for railroad keys and locks, I would find collectors who specialized in either the key or the lock. As an example, I was able to add a very early switch key (Hannibal and St. Joseph Railroad) to my collection because a switch lock collector wanted only the lock, not the key. This would have been a real find for me—a rare old railroad switch lock with its original key—but a specialist is a specialist. Alas, I am still hoping to find a Hannibal and St. Jo switch lock for my key.

Railroad markings usually are stamped on the hasp of the lock or embossed or indented on the front or back of the lock. The lock often is found with the short length of iron chain that was used to fasten it to the switch stand. The letter S stamped on the lock means "switch" and occasionally you will find the entire word spelled out. Other letters, words, numbers, and patent dates, or a manufacturer's name, also appear on these old locks. Many of them are ornate in style, others are quite plain, such as the modern switch locks used today.

Switch keys are brass, bronze, or iron, with the railroad name engraved or stamped on them. If an S is shown on the back, it is assumed to be a switch key. Other letters and numbers designate the various shops or objects for which the key was used. The manufacturer's name or patent date sometimes is stamped on the key. Besides the switch keys, there were keys to the caboose, coach, baggage car, Pullman, diner, and the lowly restroom in the coaches, where passengers would see the conductor locking the door before the train arrived at the station and unlocking it when the train pulled out again.

The rarities in switch locks and switch keys are those from the now-defunct roads, such as the "M. & P. Du C Ry." (Milwaukee and Prairie Du Chien Railway) in my collection. I also have an unusual switch key with three railroad markings on it—"UP & MP & C" (Union Pacific-Missouri Pacific-Central). Another rarity is a lock with two railroad markings, "M & I Ry." (Minnesota and International) on the hasp and "Northern Pacific" embossed across the back side of the lock. The switch key also is double-marked.

Having a set of switch locks and switch keys covering the years of a railroad's name changes ("St. Paul and Pacific RR," "St. Paul, Minneapolis and Manitoba RR," "Great Northern RR," and "Burlington Northern") is an achievement for the collector. When I look over my collection of these old switch locks and their keys, I think of all the switches that they have unlocked and locked and the many stories they could tell.

It was not too many years ago that you would see the engineer, gloved hand gripping his long-spout oilcan, standing alongside the locomotive's huge driving wheels, oiling around here and there, just before the train pulled out of the station. Of all the oilcans, kerosene cans, water cans, etc., in the railroads' "cannery department" that collectors are eagerly seeking today, the hogger's long-necked oilcan, a relic of the steam era, is the most popular of all, and is becoming harder and harder to find.

The switch tender had a different style of oilcan. Generally it was shaped like a teapot, with a short spout and a wire handle. This was used to replenish the signal oil in the switch stand lamps. (Oil-burning switch stand lamps are fast disappearing from the scene, too.) Many other types of cans were made for carrying kerosene, and there were a variety of oilcans used in shop and yard maintenance. Collectors can find these in various styles, shapes and sizes. Water cans were made in several styles, shapes, and sizes, too; some have a pouring spout and others a cover on the top. These had plenty of action by section gangs on a hot summer day.

Railroad torches also belong in this group. Some were tubular, others conical, with a wick on top, and they were held in the hand like a candle. Others resembled an upside-down funnel with a wick at the top and a long handle. These torches were for light at night while probing around the locomotive, cars, and equipment.

The railroadiana collector interested in this category will find a variety of cans and torches that were made for the railroads' use by various manufacturers down through the years. A great many of them were railroad-marked, along with the name of the manufacturer.

"I've Been Working on the Railroad" is one of the most famous of all old railroad ballads, although the songwriter is unknown. How many of us remember the familiar sight of the gandy dancers working on the tracks, digging out the old ties, replacing a section of the rail, with all their tools and equipment scattered about them? Spiking down the rail with the maul, tamping down the ties with the shovel, took muscle and sweat. It has been said that the pick and shovel built the railroad.

The sledgehammer has played a significant role in the romantic history of the building of the rails to Promontory. By the middle of 1868 the Central Pacific was crossing the Nevada desert and the Union Pacific, having crossed the continental divide, was reaching toward Wyoming. Both railroads were out to build just as many miles of track as possible. An army of gandy dancers, with their picks and shovels, raced towards each other, spiking down the rails. Each tried to outdo the other; three miles of track were laid a day, four miles, then five, six, seven miles of track a day. Charles Crocker, the Central Pacific's construction chief, boasted that his gandy dancers could lay ten miles of track in a single day. Thomas Durant, vice-president of the Union Pacific, bet him $10,000 that they couldn't do it. Crocker accepted the challenge.

On April 28, 1869 at 7:00 A.M. the race began. Not a minute was wasted as ties were put down, rails laid, spikes driven home. The Central Pacific won the bet by laying ten miles and fifty-six feet of track by quitting time at 7:00 P.M. For many years two signs were posted, one at each end of that stretch of track, reading, "10 miles of track laid in one day, April 28, 1869."

The record never has been broken. Less than a month later the golden spike was driven. The sledge that drove that golden spike is now in the Stanford Museum in Palo Alto, California.

Section gangs are becoming a thing of the past. Machinery is taking the place of muscle. A mechanized crew can do twice as much work with only half as many men and in half the time. "Track machine operators" is the new name for section crews, and many of the old tools used by the gandy dancers in the roundhouse and in the railroad shops during the steam era are no longer in use today.

Over the years railroadiana collectors have developed a growing appreciation for these old railroad tools, now that they are rapidly disappearing. Still, collectors have a good chance of finding some of these tools by searching through the accumulations of miscellaneous tools offered for sale at second-hand stores, flea markets, and garage sales. Tools that were used by the railroads usually are marked with either the railroad's name or its initials. Many also have the manufacturer's name on them and a patent date, and these are very collectible.

As passengers ride the streamlined trains of today, they may not give much thought to the roadbed over which the train glides. The wooden ties used by the American railroads if placed end to end would encircle the globe twice, with ties left over. It is scarcely surprising that they represent the largest single item of expense in the maintenance of railroads.

Around the turn of the century, the railroads began the practice of marking their ties by using a small nail with the year embossed or indented in the nailhead. The nail was pounded into the tie when it was laid. The railroads then kept a record of these date ties to determine how long they lasted, what type of wood was the best to use for ties, and what type of treatment of the wood would help make the ties last longer. Constant replacement of ties had proved to be very expensive, and the railroads were looking for an answer to this problem.

The use of date nails proved successful. The railroads discovered that treating the ties with creosote and elevating them on a roadbed of crushed stone to keep them dry made them less susceptible to frost in the northern states. Then the railroads, one after the other, stopped using date nails and, as the ties with the date nails on them deteriorated and were replaced with new, unmarked ties, the date nails began to disappear. Now they are being collected, and some of them bring top prices today.

Date nails usually bear the last two numbers of the year. Most date nails are made of iron, although some railroads used copper. The nailheads usually are round, but some square, diamond, or hexagon-shaped nails can be found. The shanks vary in length. These characteristics sometimes can be identified with specific railroads, but for most date nails, this is impossible. Many collectors simply try to see how many different dates and types of date nails they can find. This is a fairly recent area of railroadiana collecting.

The collecting of railroad medals is another interesting category. It includes many types of medals—anniversay, exhibition, safety, commemorative. And, of course, this list would not be complete without the many convention medals proudly worn by railroad employees at their Brotherhood meetings and conventions. Medals worn by old-time railroad employees are both colorful and interesting.

The large bronze anniversary medals are especially collectible. The Delaware and Hudson Railroad Company's bronze medal, rectangular in shape, and measuring 2¼ by 4 inches, shows the Stourbridge Lion on the front with the dates 1829-1929. The back of the medal reads: "Commemorating the one hundredth anniversary of the first successful trip made in America by a steam locomotive at Honesdale, Pennsylvania, August 8, 1829, by the Stourbridge Lion driven by Horatio Allen."

The Baltimore and Ohio Railroad issued a 2¾-inch-diameter round medal medal in 1927. This has Peter Cooper's Tom Thumb on one side with, "The Baltimore and Ohio Railroad Company, 1827-1927," around the edge. The other side shows a steam passenger train of the 1920s speeding down the track with a symbolic figure gliding above the locomotive. The words *One Hundred Years—Safety-Strength-Speed* circle the edge.

The Illinois Central Railroad issued a large, round bronze medal with the dates 1851-1951, to commemorate 100 years of railroad service to mid-America. The railroad's slogan, "The Main Line of Mid-America," is lettered on the bottom of the face of the medal. The back side shows a map of the United States and the railroad's lines running from Chicago to New Orleans.

Another interesting medal is a large, round bronze medal commemorating the Golden Spike Centennial Celebration. Around the edge on one side are the words *Golden Spike Centennial Celebration Commission—the oceans united by Railways.* In the middle is the golden spike with the dates 1869-1969, and the words *Sacramento, Omaha, Promontory.* The other side shows the two locomotives, the Central Pacific's Jupiter 90 and the Union Pacific's Rogers 119, meeting, and below it are the words *The Pacific Railway is completed, May 10, 1869.* Around the edge are the words *The Central Pacific and Union Pacific Railroads, linking the nation, Promontory Summit, Utah.*

The Chicago and Northwestern Railway was awarded a large, round bronze medal for safety. The front side shows a profile of Edward Harriman, and around it are the words *Edward H. Harriman Memorial Medal—awarded by the American Museum of Safety to the Chicago and North Western*

Railway Company, Group A Railroads. The other side reads, "For the utmost progress in safety and accident prevention," and it shows a man walking the tracks carrying lanterns and flags and dressed in railroad attire, representing all railroad men.

Various medals were issued for the opening of a new passenger service or a fast freight service, the completion of a branch line or the opening of an exclusive route to a resort area, and many other accomplishments. Medals were issued by various companies which manufactured products for the railroads' use. Often these pictured a locomotive and the firm's product. Usually these large, round, heavy bronze medals ended up as paperweights on a desk.

Perhaps the greatest testimonial ever given the railroad was the speech made by ninety-one-year-old Charles Carroll, one of the directors of the Baltimore and Ohio. On July 4, 1827, he turned over the first shovel of dirt at the laying of the B & O's cornerstone, and he made this statement: "I consider this among the most important acts of my life, second only to signing the Declaration of Independence, if even it be second to that."

A lot of romance is associated with the vanished steam locomotive's whistle, and to own one of these brass chimers is a fine addition to any collection.

A builder's plate is the birth certificate of every locomotive. Pictured here is the locomotive and the plate it bore throughout its lifetime.

M. St. P. & S. Ste. M. Ry.
175691
BUILT AT
SHOREHAM SHOPS
JAN. 1930

Like the cowboy and his Stetson, the trainman and his cap were always together in his line of duty.

A framed collection of railroad men's cap badges.

The shiny gold-and-silver buttons on the railroad man's uniform always caught the eye of the passenger.

Pinbacks were widely worn down through the years by railroad employees. These are becoming harder and harder to find.

An attractive breast badge, no doubt worn proudly by its owner.

A grouping of breast badges worn by men who worked on the railroad.

Way back when, railroad timekeepers were widely advertised, as shown in this attractive tin sign. The watch in the center is a Rockford.

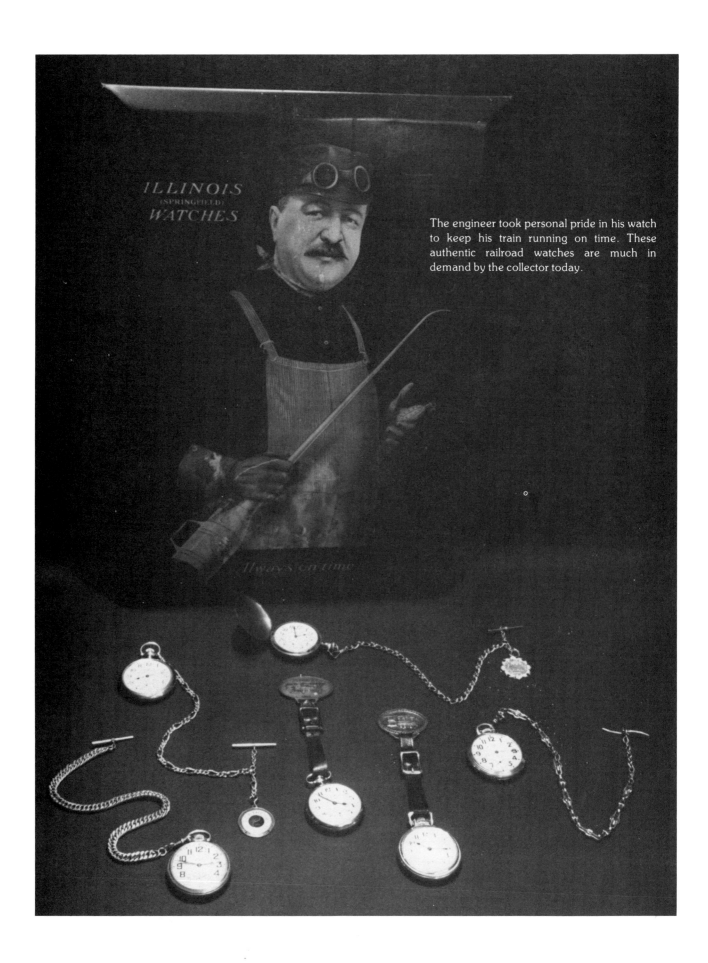

The engineer took personal pride in his watch to keep his train running on time. These authentic railroad watches are much in demand by the collector today.

A Trainmen's Special watch with a locomotive on the dial captured the imagination of many railroad men, but these were not always approved railroad watches.

Many railroad men's old watches had engravings of a locomotive on the back side of the case. Here's a real beauty.

The Seth Thomas clock was a familiar fixture on the depot walls back in those days.
These now have become scarce.

A rare event for the collector is to find an early railroad hand lantern. This one from the Atlantic and St. Lawrence R.R. dates back to the 1860s.

Hand lamp used by the railroad car inspector as he made his rounds.

The conductor's classic hand lantern of yesterday was proudly shown off when he was promoted to conductor. Some were gleaming brass, others nickel-plated. The lantern in the center has a two-color globe, green over clear.

188

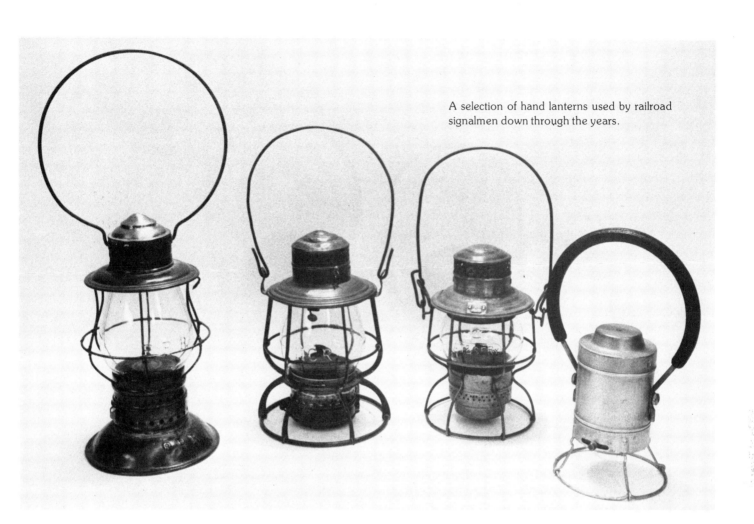

A selection of hand lanterns used by railroad signalmen down through the years.

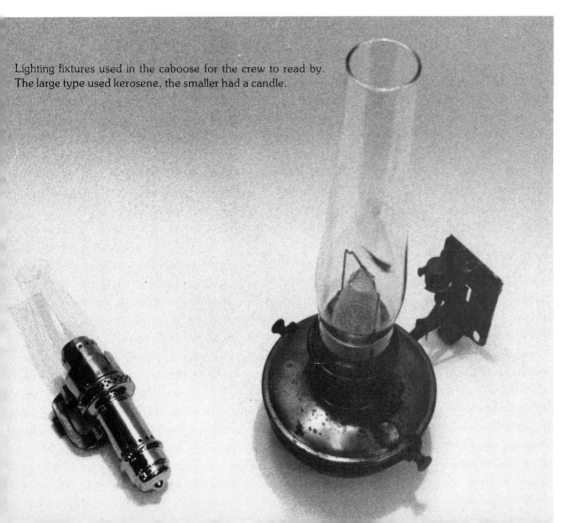

Lighting fixtures used in the caboose for the crew to read by. The large type used kerosene, the smaller had a candle.

189

This oil-burning headlight lit the way for the Iron Horse back in the early days.

Electric headlights took over when the flame was extinguished.

A pair of caboose marker lamps. These were the taillights for the freight train.

Switch-stand lamps made the rail yards look like Christmas Eve at night during the winter with their display of red, green, and yellow lights. Those used during the steam era are much in demand by the collector today.

Candles were used in the early days to provide the light for the colored lens in the semaphore signal lamps. Here is one—a rarity.

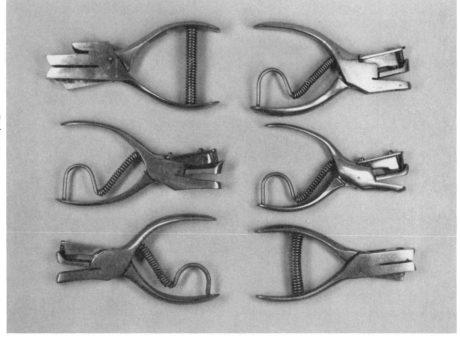

Conductor's ticket punches came in many styles and die designs for punching the passenger's tickets. Here are some.

The telegraph operator's key, sounder, and relay played a vital role in running the trains. Most of these have vanished from the scene and are much sought after by collectors today.

Glass insulators used on the singing wires stretching between the telephone poles from station to station are now being collected. These three are railroad marked.

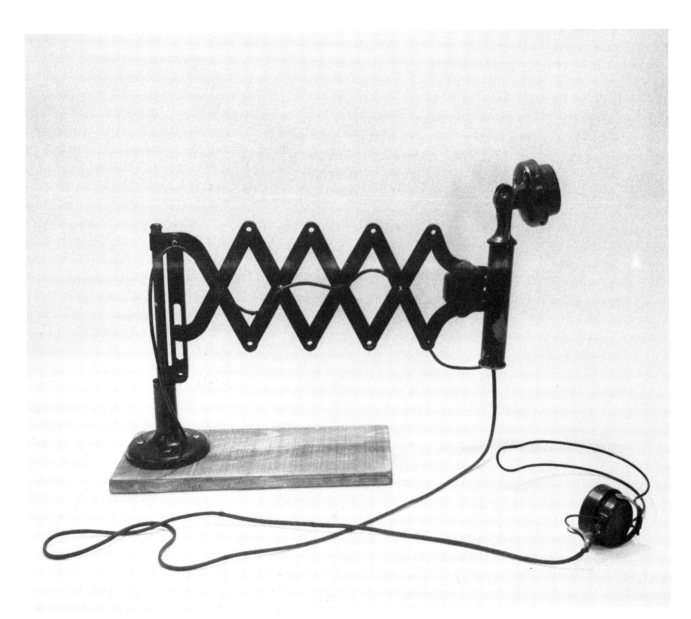

The elusive scissors phone was part of every railroad station's equipment down through the years. Still in service today on some railroads, they are becoming difficult to locate.

Old station wall phones and bell boxes used by the dispatcher in the old days are no longer easy to come by.

The railroad lineman had a portable phone, which he took with him when he climbed up the telephone pole, connecting it to the wires to place his call. Here is one from the old days.

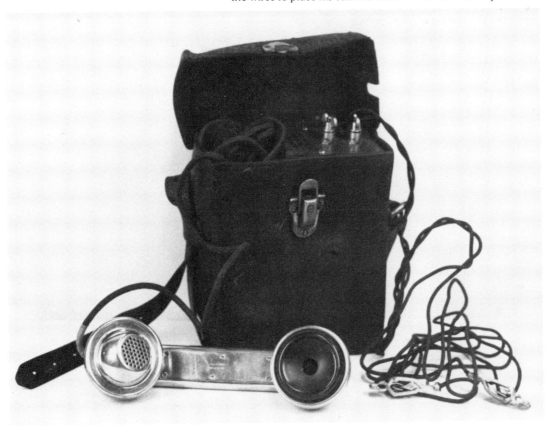

Wax sealers showing the reverse lettering in the matrix.

Wax sealers were used by the railroads to safeguard envelopes years ago. Shown here is a wax sealer, a stick of sealing wax, spirits torch to melt the wax, and the wax impressions on the envelope.

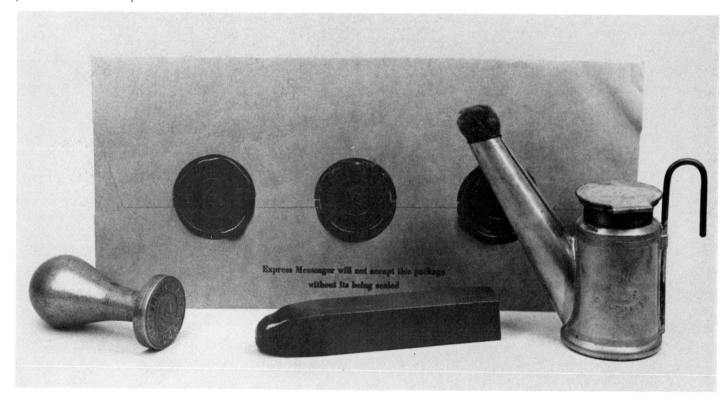

A display of railroad wax sealers showing the various types of handles on them, both wood and metal. This is a specialized field for many railroadiana collectors.

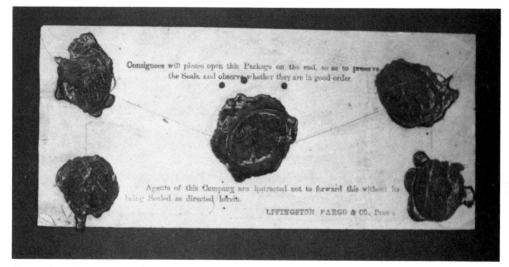

Original early money-package envelopes with the original wax seals still intact are very rare and highly prized by the wax sealer collector.

A collection of old railroad switch and signal locks.

A station agent's door key.

A collection of old railroad switch keys can be attractively displayed mounted on a wall frame.

Two oil cans and a kerosene can from the
railroad's cannery department.

Hand torches were in common use by the
railroad men during the days of steam.

Engineer's classic long-spout oil cans of the steam era have virtually disappeared from the scene.

Galvanized water cans got much use in quenching the thirst of railroad men on hot summer days.

An old pottery drinking-water jug used by the enginemen in the cab.

The fireman's coal scoop has now taken its place among railroadiana collectibles.

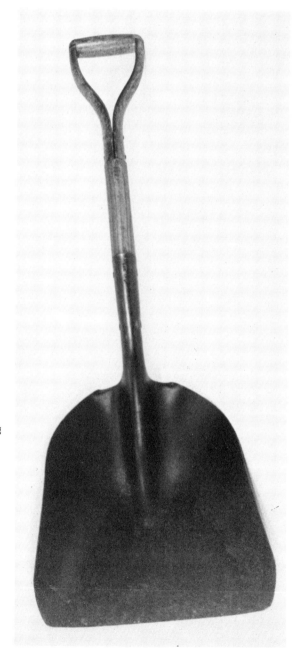

These brass tokens used in the early days at fuel stops to buy wood were as good as cash when redeemed at the railroad companies' offices. They are very rare.

The once-overlooked date nail has now come into its own. Collectors are busy seeking them out and classifying them.

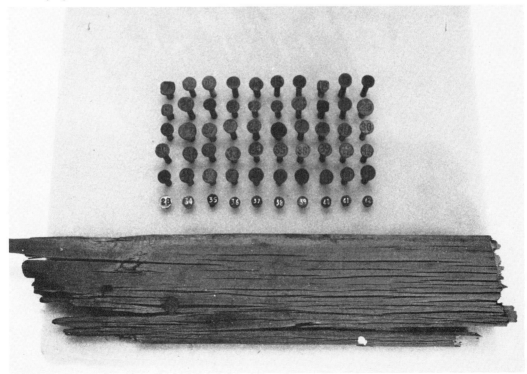

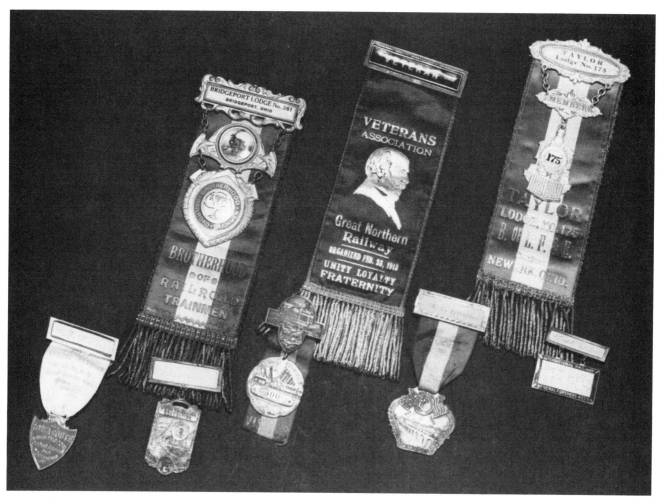

Some of the Brotherhood and Convention medals, which were proudly worn by their owners in the good old days.

One Hundredth Anniversary medal of the Baltimore and Ohio railroad showing Peter Cooper's Tom Thumb.

The back side of the B & O medal, showing their modern passenger train with a symbolic figure above it.

The Chicago & Northwestern Railroad was awarded this medal by the American Museum of Safety. It bears a profile of Edward H. Harriman.

The back side of the Harriman Memorial medal.

The Delaware and Hudson Railroad issued this medal in 1929 to commemorate the centennial of the first running of the Stourbridge Lion.

Tools that built the railroad—pick, shovel, and spiking maul.

Railroad Museums

Note: This is a representative sampling of some of the many railroad museums. The hours, admission prices, and opening and closing dates listed below are subject to change. It would be wise to call or write for verification in advance of your visit.

CALIFORNIA

CALIFORNIA RAILWAY MUSEUM, Rio Vista
(Operated by the Bay Area Electric Railroad Association)
2119 Marin Avenue
Berkeley, CA 94707
(707) 374-2978

Location: The museum is on State Rte 12, halfway between Fairfield and Rio Vista Junction (approximately twelve miles from both of them), where State Highway 12 passes over the Sacramento Northern Railway. From San Francisco and Oakland, take I-80 to the Fairfield turnoff, and State Rte 12 to Rio Vista Junction.

Hours and Rates: Open year round, Saturday and Sunday, noon to 5 P.M. Admission to museum, picnic area, and parking is free. Old-time fare boxes at various locations are reminders to give what you can. Fares for rides: Adults $1.50, children $.75. Tickets are good for unlimited rides on the day of sale.

Features: The museum contains a diversity of equipment, both steam and electric, the rolling stock having been acquired from many sources. Much of the historic equipment is operated over a one-and-a-quarter-mile line traversing the museum grounds.

COLORADO

COLORADO RAILROAD MUSEUM
P.O. Box 10
Golden, CO 80401
(303) 279-4591

Location: The museum is located at the foot of North Table Mountain, just two miles east of the center of Golden and twelve miles west of downtown Denver. To reach it, go straight out Interstate 70 to Exit 63, then just minutes further on West 44th Avenue.

Hours and Rates: Open daily year round, 9 A.M. to 5 P.M. Adults $1.25, children $.50; or family of parents and their children under sixteen, $2.95.

Features: The museum building, a replica of an 1880-style masonry railroad depot, houses rare old papers, photos, and artifacts displayed so as to give the viewer an accurate insight into the interesting histories of the various roads. Outside, displayed on authentic track layouts beneath Table Mountain, is an extensive collection of narrow gauge and standard gauge locomotives, cars, and other railroadiana, dating from the 1870s to the present era. The museum carries one of the largest stocks of railroadiana in the West. Catalogs and auction lists are sent with the free *Iron Horse News* several times yearly; send six self-addressed, stamped #10 envelopes.

ILLINOIS

ILLINOIS RAILWAY MUSEUM
P.O. Box 431
Union, IL 60180
(815) 923-2488

Location: From Chicago, take the Illinois Northwest Tollway (I-90) to U.S. 20, Marengo exit. Drive northwest on U.S. 20, about four and a half miles, to Union Road. Drive northeast on Union one mile through town (on Jefferson Street) to Olson Road. Turn south to the museum.

Hours and Rates: Open daily, 10 A.M. to 5 P.M., June 15 through Labor Day. Free admission and free parking. Rides: Adults $1.00, children $.50.

Features: The museum is the world's largest operating railway museum, with forty-six acres of outdoor display as a setting for over 140 steam engines, streetcars, interurban cars, elevated railway cars, steam railroad cars, and trolley buses. There are a dozen old Chicago and Milwaukee streetcars, interurban trains from the North Shore Line and Chicago, Aurora & Elgin, as well as ten steam engines. If all this equipment were coupled together in one train, it would be over a mile and a half long. Several pieces of this equipment are operated over the museum's demonstration railway. The present line is one and one-quarter miles long, with another four miles to be constructed in the future.

The museum displays and gift shop are located at their 1851 railway depot (the oldest railway depot west of Pittsburgh). Here you can purchase soda pop, color postcards, books, and other railroad-oriented items—or just browse.

INDIANA

INDIANA RAILWAY MUSEUM
Box 258
Greensburg, IN 47240
(812) 663-8259

Location: Exit Interstate 74 at the Greensburg/Indiana Route 3 South interchange, turn right at Keillor's Restaurant (10th Street), right again at Broadway, and continue north to the museum.

Schedule: Trains depart Greensburg at 12:00 P.M., 2:00 P.M, and 4:00 P.M. EST on Saturdays, Sundays, and Monday holidays (May 31, July 5, September 6) from May 29 through October 31. Donation: Adults $2.50, children under fourteen $1.50, under three, free. Refreshments, souvenirs, and rest rooms on site. Free parking.

Features: Steam engine Number 11 and ex-Milwaukee Road and Erie Railroad coaches make nine-mile, hour-long round trips throughout the summer months, recreating the classic American branch line local passenger train. Also on display at the museum are examples of several different types of freight and passenger cars.

MAINE

BOOTHBAY RAILWAY MUSEUM
Route 27
Boothbay, ME

Location: Located on Rte 27, just before the entrance to the town of Boothbay, and just ten minutes from picturesque Boothbay Harbor. In addition to the museum, the immediate area offers a motel, camping area, service station, and drive-in restaurants.

Hours and Rates: Open daily from 10 A.M. Memorial Day through September. Adults $.75, children $.50.

Features: The museum is housed in two restored railroad stations, one moved from Freeport, Maine, the other from Thorndike, Maine. Throughout the buildings are many displays of the various items used in or pertaining to the steam railroading era that was so essential to the building of our country. There is one of the last remaining narrow gauge railroad rides in America; enjoy a pleasant and entertaining trip on the Boothbay Central, behind a real steam locomotive.

The Boothbay Junction General Store, adjacent to the railway station, offers many interesting items of a bygone era. There are free picnic grounds throughout the area surrounding the museum, and snacks are available at the Depot Lunch. Be sure to visit the standard gauge caboose, once in actual use on the Maine Central Railroad.

MARYLAND

BALTIMORE & OHIO TRANSPORTATION MUSEUM
Pratt and Poppleton Streets
Baltimore, MD 21223
(301) 237-3821

Location: Located on the western edge of downtown Baltimore.

Hours and Rates: Open Wednesday through Sunday (except on major holidays) from 10 A.M. to 4 P.M. Admission: $1.50 for adults, $.75 for children twelve and under; group rates available on request.

Features: The museum houses a unique collection of cars and locomotives dating back to 1829. The entrance to the museum is through the old Mt. Clare Station, built in 1830, the first railroad passenger depot in the United States, now completely restored. There is an agent's office, reconstructed as it was in the 1850s. The Roundhouse, built in 1884, now houses the world's largest array of original railroad equipment. Included in the newly restored structure are a "grasshopper," built in 1832; the elegant "William Mason," a 4-4-0 of 1856; an 1873 "Camel"; the "J. C. Davis," first passenger Mogul and a star of the Centennial Exposition of the United States in Philadelphia in 1876. There is an operating HO gauge model railroad and a delightful display of antique toy trains. The famous B & O gift shop offers a varied selection of railroad items for sale.

MASSACHUSETTS

EDAVILLE RAILROAD MUSEUM
P.O. Box 77, Route 58
South Carver, MA 02566
(617) 866-4526

Location: On Rte 58, just off the major routes to and from Cape Cod. Stop 5 on the Americana Trail; follow the signs.

Hours: Spring: April and May. Sundays and holidays, noon to 5 P.M.
Summer: June 5 through Labor Day. Monday through Saturday, 10 A.M. to 5:30 P.M. Sundays, noon to 5:30 P.M.
Fall: September 7 through October 31. Weekdays, 10:30 A.M. to 3 P.M. (Diesel); Saturdays, Sundays, and holidays, noon to 5 P.M. (steam).
Winter: November 7, 11, 14, noon to 4 P.M. November 19 through January 2, weekdays 4 P.M. to 9 P.M., weekends 2 P.M. to 9 P.M. Closed Thanksgiving and Christmas Day.

Rates: Adults $2.50, children under twelve $1.25. Includes admission to grounds and train ride. Combination tickets (train and museum): Adults $3.00, children $1.50. Open rain or shine.

Features: Live a little history by visiting the famous historic narrow gauge steam railroad, riding through Cape Cod cranberry country, a five-and-one-half-mile Iron Horse trail on an authentic steam train, reliving the golden days of America's narrow gauge railroading. When your train arrives back at Edaville center, visit the famous Edaville Museum; there you will see one of the nation's finest collections of railroadiana, which includes the prestigious Railway and Locomotive Historical Society collection.

MINNESOTA

LAKE SUPERIOR MUSEUM of TRANSPORTATION & INDUSTRY
506 W. Michigan Street
Duluth, MN 55802
(218) 727-8025

Location: The museum is located at the Depot, corner of 5th Avenue West and Michigan Street, Duluth, Minnesota.

Rates and Hours: Guided tours are conducted 10 A.M. to 5 P.M. Monday through Saturday, in June, July, August, and September. Adults $.50, children (six-twelve) $.25.

Features: Started in 1890 and opened on March 1, 1892, the Union Depot is considered to be one of the finest examples of French Norman architecture in the United States. When passenger service to Duluth ended in 1969, it was named a National Historical Site in 1971 and preserved. In its heyday the Union Depot served seven railroads, with fifty trains arriving and departing every day. See the famous William Crooks, Minnesota's first locomotive and train, 1862; The Little 1870 Minnetonka, the first locomotive to operate in the Duluth area; the Giant Mallet, the world's most powerful steam locomotive; and, in addition, an extensive collection of locomotives, cars, and memorabilia depicting railroading's golden era, including locomotive headlights, bells, marker and switch lamps, old timetables, maps, and much more.

OHIO

Conneaut Railroad Museum
Conneaut, OH 44030

Location: Just off SR 20 or IS 90. Follow the railroad museum signs.

Hours and Rates: Open daily 10 A.M. to 6 P.M., Memorial Day through Labor Day. Admission free, donations accepted.

Features: The former New York Central depot, built in 1900, is the home of the Conneaut Railroad Museum. Besides rare items, such as an 1866 stock certificate of the Red River Line (NYC) and relics from the Ashtabula Bridge Disaster of 1876, are large displays of lanterns, timetables, passes, and old photos. There are several large-scale models of locomotives and equipment, along with smaller gauge models. There are many other items that were used during the steam era. Refreshments and some unusual souvenirs are available at the snack-souvenir bar.

Ohio Railway Museum
990 Proprietors Road
P.O. Box 171
Worthington, OH 43085

Location: The museum is just north of Rte 161 in Worthington. It may be reached from Rte 23 (turn east on Rte 161, then north at the second traffic light) or from I-71 (turn west at the Worthington–New Albany exit, then north at the third traffic light).

Hours and Rates: Electric equipment is operated for the public from 1 P.M. to 5 P.M. on Saturdays from June through August, and from 12:30 P.M. to 5:30 P.M. Sundays from May through October. Other equipment is operated when conditions warrant. Tickets for rides are available at nominal amounts. Children under five are free. Special charter runs of about an hour's duration may be arranged for groups: write to Mrs. Karl Walters, 882 Chambers Road, Columbus, OH, phone (614) 486-2265.

Features: The museum, founded in 1948, is dedicated to the preservation and operation of historical railway equipment. Members have constructed one and a half miles of main line, six sidings, a bridge, substation, car barn, and passenger station and have restored over twenty pieces of equipment, both steam and electric. Besides an authentic operating railway signal system, the museum has a full-size reproduction of a small-town depot representing railroad architecture of the 1890s era. Erected as a result of donations of labor and funds by members and friends, this building houses museum offices, a gift shop, public facilities, and an exhibit of historical items of railroad interest.

PENNSYLVANIA

Railways to Yesterday, Orbisonia
328 North 28th Street
Allentown, PA 18104
(814) 447-3011 (weekends only)

Location: Located at Orbisonia on Rte 522, just thirty minutes north of Pennsylvania Turnpike exits 13 or 14.

Hours: June, weekends. July and August, every day. September and October, weekends. Trains run on the hour, 11 A.M. to 4 P.M.

Features: On the East Broad Top Railroad you can ride behind steam on a ten-mile, fifty-minute round trip, one of the oldest narrow gauge lines in America. This is the last three-foot gauge line in the east still operating in its original location. Built in 1873, the East Broad Top was designed for the movement of coal from the Broad Top mines of Central Pennsylvania to Mt. Union. In 1964 it was designated a Registered National Historic Landmark by the U.S. National Park Service.

Begin your day at the East Broad Top by visiting the original eight-stall roundhouse and inspecting the steam locomotives. Photograph the engine being readied for the day's operation as it pauses on the Armstrong turntable, and browse through Orbisonia station for film, souvenirs, and refreshments. Then purchase your ticket and board the train for a fifty-minute journey through the picturesque Aughwick Valley. At the end of the line the entire train will turn around on the wye, and there, if you wish, you may stop over at Colgate Grove, the picnic area. Take any later train back to the station. Directly across from the station is the Shade Gap Electric Railway, the trolley that meets the East Broad Top steam trains.

LAKE SHORE RAILWAY HISTORICAL SOCIETY, INC.
P.O. Box 571
North East, PA 16428

Location: Take Interstate 90 to exit 12, then go west on W.S. 20 to Robinson Street and south on Robinson to Wall. The museum is located on the corner of Wall and Robinson.

Hours and Rates: Open to the public on Saturdays, Sundays, and holidays, May through September, 1 P.M. to 5 P.M., and other times by appointment. Because there is no admission fee, fare boxes have been placed in display areas for contributions.

Features: Since May, 1970, the Lake Shore Railway Historical Society has operated a public railroad museum at the former New York Central passenger depot here. Inside the station are a host of interesting displays of railroad items. Many old photographs of area railroads are framed along with reproductions of paintings commissioned by railroads and locomotive builders. There are hand signal lanterns hung throughout the interior. One display counter is filled with the many small items once found in passenger trains. One may sit in the old waiting room on benches used in the old Nickel Plate station in nearby Erie. Outside the museum, volunteers are building track for full-sized railroad equipment. There are also plans to set up an old-time elevated watchman's shanty, which once stood about a half mile east of the station on the NYC, plus one or two old-style signals. The society is dedicated to the preservation of historical railroad items. Many of these are maintained for public viewing at the museum station.

TENNESSEE

TENNESSEE VALLEY RAILROAD MUSEUM
P.O. Box 5263
Chattanooga, TN 37406
(615) 622-5908, 265-8861

Location: The museum is located at 2202 North Chamberlain Avenue, just ten minutes drive from downtown Chattanooga.

Hours and Rates: Admission to the museum is $1.00 for adults and $.50 for children through twelve. Admission includes the display tour and two round trips over the railroad. There is no charge for TVRM members. Arrangements may be made for train rides for special groups at any time during the week, including meals in the diner if desired. Phone or write for details.

Features: Every Sunday afternoon between May 9 and October the museum is open to the public for tours through the displays and for train rides. The museum contains the finest collection of railroad equipment from the golden age of steam railroading in the Southeast. More than thirty-five items are on display, and many may be seen in actual operation. Included are pullmans, mail cars, baggage cars, streetcars, a caboose, and a diner, together with a variety of steam, electric, Diesel, and gasoline-powered locomotives.

The three-mile, forty-five minute round trips are usually behind a steam engine, although other types of power may be used on occasion. These trips include a ride through historic Missionary Ridge tunnel, a visit to a nature park which is accessible only by train, and a ride through the workshop area where cars and locomotives are being restored. Also included in the tours are the gift shop, the waiting room, the rest room car, and the dining car, which serves snacks and refreshments.

CASEY JONES HOME RAILROAD MUSEUM
P.O. Box 682
Jackson, TN 38301
(901) 427-8382

Location: The museum is located at 211 West Chester Street, Jackson, and is owned and operated by the City of Jackson.

Hours and Rates: Open to the public Mondays through Saturdays, 9 A.M. to 4 P.M. and Sundays, 1 P.M. to 4 P.M., subject to change. Closed legal holidays. Free parking lot and souvenir gift shop.

Features: Casey Jones was residing in the cottage that now houses the museum at the time of his death at the throttle of *Old 382,* on the Illinois Central Railroad at Vaughan, Mississippi, April 30, 1900. The museum is the glorification of the age of steam on the rails. It contains old pictures and prints of early American railroads—old railroad passes, historic timetables, early dining car menus, telegraph instruments, railroad money, lanterns, steam whistles, old railroad ballads, scrapbooks, clippings, and prints dealing with railroads from the earliest day.

Now on display is a colorful "six-eight-Wheeler," as the songwriter misnamed this high-speed engine of 1900, the same type that carried Casey Jones to his death. The whippoorwill whistle on display in the museum was made by Casey's son, Charlie, an exact duplicate of the old "whippoorwill" that Casey was blowing at the time of the wreck—the whistle that won fame in song and story.

TEXAS

PATE MUSEUM OF TRANSPORTATION
P.O. Box 711
Fort Worth, TX 78101
(817) 332-1161, 396-2811

Location: The museum is located on U.S. Highway 377 between Fort Worth and Cresson, Texas.

Hours and Rates: Open daily, 9 A.M. to 5 P.M., except Mondays. Free admission.

Features: Exhibits at the museum range from a covered wagon to space travel. Railroad exhibits acquired by the museum are growing in number almost daily. The pride and joy of the rail exhibits at the museum is the *Sunshine Special's Ellsmere.* The *Ellsmere* is an antique, private railcar built in

1914 by the Pullman Corporation for Dr. William Seward Webb, a former president of the Wagner Palace Car Company. Later the *Ellsmere* was acquired by the Texas and Pacific Railroad and used as a president's car until retired to the Pate Museum. Other rail exhibits include model trains, china, linens, and photos of some of the famous trains in United States history.

The Pate Museum of Transportation has rapidly become a foremost attraction in the Southwest. For young and old there are exhibits galore. And you can't beat the price of admission anywhere!

VERMONT

STEAMTOWN FOUNDATION
P.O. Box 71
Bellows Falls, VT 05101
(802) 463-3937

Location: On U.S. Rte 5, South Interstate 91, exit 6, two miles north of the Village of Bellows Falls.

Train Schedule: May 29 to June 26: Saturday, Sunday, and holidays,   11:35, 1:35, 3:35
June 26 to September 6: Daily   11:35, 1:35, 3:35
September 11 to September 26: Saturday and Sunday,   11:35, 1:35, 3:35
September 27 to October 17: Monday through Friday,   1:35,
Saturday, Sunday, and holidays,   11:35, 1:35, 3:35
Museum grounds open daily, May 24 to October 22.

Rates: Adults $5.50, children ages two to eleven $2.95. One ticket admits you to all activities, including one round-trip train ride (one and a quarter hours), the exhibit area, free movies, the picnic area, and parking. There are food and gift shops on the premises. Tickets are on sale only at Steamtown.

Features: The Steamtown Museum collection is the world's largest collection of steam locomotives and equipment. Steamtown is working toward the goal of becoming the world's finest railroad museum, with many more locomotives operating and exhibits attractively displayed and preserved, a kind of living history of the days of steam. On adjacent tracks around the museum are numerous other exhibits: once-elegant passenger cars, cabooses, giant steam cranes, museum cars displaying railroad artifacts, and more. You will enjoy strolling around the grounds and examining these great old giants of the past. Take a nostalgic train ride behind a real, full-size steam locomotive over some of the most scenic and historic trackage in Vermont. The path of these former Rutland Railroad tracks is older than any historical record. The whistle blows, the bell rings, and the big locomotive is on its way, the conductor calling out the things to see and recreating the feeling of the era of steam.

VIRGINIA

ROANOKE TRANSPORTATION MUSEUM
Wasena Park
Roanoke, VA 24016
(703) 981-2236

Location: In Wasena Park, on the Roanoke River.

Hours and Rates: Opens Memorial Day and closes Labor Day. Tuesday through Sunday, 1 P.M. to 7 P.M. Admission $.25.

Features: The museum is owned by the City of Roanoke and operated by its department of parks and recreation. Founded in 1963, the museum has become the largest municipally owned facility of this type in the United States. It houses the most extensive collection of railroad historical materials south of Baltimore and east of St. Louis. Since Roanoke is the home of the Norfolk and Western Railway Company, the city is proud that it can preserve many samples of railroading equipment prominent in the development of the community. Relics of the High Rails consist of Norfolk and Western: Virginian; Nickel Plate: Wabash; C & O: Southern—the South's largest collection of fabulous fabled "Iron Horses" of steam railroading days.

Visit the old mail car, concession stand, and picnic area. In the special children's area, press a button and hear the history of exhibits. There is continual train music of old engine sounds.

WASHINGTON

PUGET SOUND AND SNOQUALMIE VALLEY RAILROAD, Snoqualmie
Puget Sound Railway Historical Association, Inc.
P.O. Box 3801
Seattle, WA 98124
(206) 888-0373

Location: At Snoqualmie, Washington, 27 miles east of Seattle, on I-90, Snoqualmie Falls exit, left at first light. No. 210 Issaquah-North Bend bus can be taken from downtown Seattle.

Schedule: (leaving from Snoqualmie Depot): Trains leave hourly—10 A.M. to 5 P.M. Sundays and holidays, April 4 through September 6; Saturdays, July 3 through September 4. Fares, adults: $2.00; children (sixteen and under) and senior citizens (sixty-five and older): $1.00; infants free. Length of round-trip train ride, seven miles. Tour of museum site included.

The Puget Sound Railroad Museum is operated by the Puget Sound Railway Historical Association, Inc., founded in 1957 to preserve and operate Pacific Northwest steam and electric railway equipment. The historical collection includes many steam locomotives, freight and passenger cars, interurbans, trolleys, steam cranes, and railway speeder cars.

WISCONSIN

NATIONAL RAILROAD MUSEUM
2285 South Broadway
Green Bay, WI 54304
(414) 432-0565

Hours and Rates: Open weekends May 1 through May 28, 9 A.M. to 5 P.M. Open daily May 29 through October 3, 9 A.M. to 5 P.M. Open weekends the balance of October, 9 A.M. to 5 P.M. Midweek visits in October and November by special appointment. Admission rates: Adults $2.00, children over six $1.00. Group rates: Adults $1.75, children over six $.75. These rates include guided tours and ride on a standard gauge train when operating.

Features: A visit to the National Railroad Museum is akin to living in a steam-age wonderland. Historic locomotives and cars are exhibited in a beautiful park on the banks of the Fox River. Exhibited inside the old-fashioned depot is a collection of hundreds of railroad accessories used to keep the trains rolling during the steam age. A library with volumes of books and literature pertaining to early railroading is available for reference and research. Additional displays of historic equipment and accessories are constantly being added. A visit is a memorable experience.

MID-CONTINENT RAILWAY MUSEUM
North Freedom, WI 53951
(608) 522-8805

Location: The museum is only fifteen minutes away from the Circus World Museum, Baraboo, and thirty minutes from Wisconsin Dells.

Hours and Rates: Open daily 10:30 A.M. to 6:00 P.M. May 29 through Labor Day. Saturdays and Sundays only through October 17. Adults $2.75, children $1.25. Group admissions of twenty to fifty persons: Adults $2.50, children $1.15. More than fifty persons: Adults $2.35, children $1.10. Special charter trips can be arranged during the operating season.

Features: Admission includes a nine-mile round-trip steam train ride, a walking tour guide pamphlet, and entrance to all exhibits, open equipment, and displays. The train ride takes about one hour. Picnic tables are available to museum visitors on the museum grounds in Pine Tree Park, next to the depot. Gifts, souvenirs, postcards, and soft drinks are available at the museum's depot. Camping facilities are available at several private campgrounds in the area or at Devil's Lake State Park

The Mid-Continent Railway is an authentic replica of a typical American steam-powered shortline railroad of the turn-of-the-century era. Lovingly restored antique steam locomotives and coaches make up an old-time train that runs on a nine-mile, hour-long scenic round trip to yesteryear through the historic iron-mining ghost town of LaRue. Trains depart from the Walnut Street Depot at 11 A.M., 12:30 P.M., 2 P.M., 3:30 P.M., and 5 P.M. Special Saturday evening moonlight train rides at 7:30 in July and August.

CANADA

CANADIAN RAILWAY MUSEUM
Canadian Railway Historical Association
P.O. Box C.P. 148
St. Constant, Quebec, Canada
(514) 632-2410.

Location: The entrance to the museum is located at 122A St. Pierre Street, St. Constant, ten miles from Montreal and about thirty miles from the United States border. From downtown Montreal go across the Mercier bridge, then east along route 9C, turning right at the second stoplight. From the United States border follow route 9 toward Montreal, then take exit marked 9C/Mercier Bridge, and turn left at the second traffic light.

Hours and Rates: Open mid-May to Labor Day, then weekends only until the end of October, 10 A.M. to 5 P.M. Adults $1.50; children $.75.

Features: The Canadian Railway Museum has the largest collection of railway equipment in North America. Most of the equipment on display is enclosed in two major exhibit buildings, including more than thirty-five steam locomotives from various Canadian railways. There are more than a hundred pieces of equipment on display, including steam, Diesel, and electric locomotives; freight and passenger cars; streetcars and interurban cars. Streetcar and caboose rides are offered on Sunday throughout the summer season. The John Molson is an operating replica of an 1849 steam locomotive and runs on selected weekends. There is also train service on holidays throughout the museum season. Facilities include picnic tables and a gift shop.

National Railway Historical Society Chapters

The National Railway Historical Society has over a hundred chapters throughout the United States. Their main headquarters is in Philadelphia, PA 19103 (Box 2051). Listed below is their current roster giving the names and addresses of the local chapters by states, for readers' ready reference.

ALABAMA

ALABAMA GULF
S. J. Smitherman
501 Willowbrook Run East
Mobile, AL 36605

HEART OF DIXIE
Wm. A. Boone
509 South 10th Avenue
Birmingham, AL 35205

MONTGOMERY
Z. S. Powers
3384 Cloverdale Road
Montgomery, AL 36106

WIREGRASS
A. J. Register
R.D. 8, Box 25
Dothan, AL 36301

ALASKA

ALASKA-YUKON
William Thomasson
P.O. Box 2248
Anchorage, AK 99501

ARIZONA

ARIZONA
Sheldon Schwedler
1544 East Cypress
Phoenix, AZ 85006

OLD PUEBLO
Earl Spaeth
1209 West Edgewater Drive
Tucson, AZ 85704

ARKANSAS

LITTLE ROCK
Clifton E. Hull
203 East 16th Street
North Little Rock, AR 72114

CALIFORNIA

CENTRAL COAST
Donald Tustin
P.O. Box 8407
San Jose, CA 95155

COLORADO

COLORADO MIDLAND
T. E. Daniels
1323 Server Drive
Colorado Springs, CO 80910

INTERMOUNTAIN
Rev. G. S. Barnes
1475 South Humboldt Street
Denver, CO 80210

CONNECTICUT

CONNECTICUT VALLEY
Wm. E. Wood
1625 North Street
Suffield, CT 06078

WESTERN CONNECTICUT
Robert Gambling
P.O. Box 724 (Belden Station)
Norwalk, CT 06852

DELAWARE

WILMINGTON
Thomas H. Smith
509 Baynard Boulevard
Wilmington, DE 19803

FLORIDA

CENTRAL FLORIDA
Clayton Bishop
419 South Grove
Eustis, FL 32726

JACKSONVILLE
R. C. Oehmer, Jr.
3211 Cristo Lane
Jacksonville, FL 32211

GULF WIND
Raymond J. Lewis
3917 Cates Avenue
Tallahassee, FL 32304

MIAMI
Robert M. Bader
10500 S.W. 82nd Avenue
Miami, FL 33156

PALM BEACHES
Ronald Kuiken
142 S.W. 9th Avenue
Boynton Beach, FL 33435

TAMPA BAY
Russ Schwartz
1354 Eastfield Drive
Clearwater, FL 33516

GEORGIA

ATLANTA
James Brooks
P.O. Box 203
East Point, GA 30344

CHATTOHOOCHEE VALLEY
Victor L. Burns
6113 Arnold Drive
Midland, GA 31820

AUGUSTA
Scott Nixon
627 Scott's Way
Augusta, GA 30904

COOSA VALLEY
Dr. Edward Flowers
103 John Maddox Drive
Rome, GA 30161

HAWAII

HAWAII
Dr. Robert Kemble
2063 Makiki Street
Honolulu, HI 96822

ILLINOIS

BLACKHAWK
F. Clayton Snyder
6633 North Drake
Lincolnwood, IL 60645

NORTHWESTERN ILLINOIS
J. Fredrickson
2130 Forest View Road
Rockford, IL 61108

DANVILLE JUNCTION
Richard Schroeder
1116 Saratoga Drive
Danville, IL 61832

OVERLAND
Robert L. Decker
1720-4th Street
Moline, IL 61265

INDIANA

INDIANAPOLIS
R. A. Frederick
8417 Lindburgh Drive
Indianapolis, IN 46239

IOWA

IOWA
Maxon P. Roller
Box 194, R.D. 1
Bettendorf, IA 52722

KANSAS

TOPEKA
Robert Balzer
1228 Woodward
Topeka, KS 66604

WICHITA
David Lawrence
3234 North Coolidge
Wichita, KS 67204

KENTUCKY

LOUISVILLE
William Mayer
4027 Busath Avenue
Louisville, KY 40218

OWENSBORO
Joseph S. Wirth
1908 Cecelia Court
Owensboro, KY 42301

LOUISIANA

NEW ORLEANS
Arthur Retif
5530 St. Claude Avenue
New Orleans, LA 70117

SOUTH EAST LOUISIANA
T. D. Corzine
1496 South Peck
Baton Rouge, LA 70808

MARYLAND

BALTIMORE
John R. Eicker
322 East 25th Street
Baltimore, MD 21218

POTOMAC
Ara Mesrobian
7410 Connecticut Avenue
Chevy Chase, MD 20015

MASSACHUSETTS

BOSTON
Lawson K. Hill
163 Moffat Road
Waban, MA 02168

CAPE COD
Thomas Annin
P.O. Box 478
South Yarmouth, MA 02664

NARRAGANSETT BAY
David Derow
8 College Avenue
Arlington, MA 02174

MICHIGAN

WEST MICHIGAN
Charles A. Rogers, Sr.
1817 Palace S.W.
Grand Rapids, MI 49509

MINNESOTA

NORTH STAR
Robert O. Macnie
3135 Casco Circle
Wayzata, MN 55391

MISSISSIPPI

CASEY JONES
Ben Pettis
1106 South Lamar
Oxford, MS 39440

MISS GREAT SOUTHERN
Sam Lindsey, Jr.
1810 North 7th Avenue
Laurel, MS 39440

MISSOURI

KANSAS CITY
Jack Morgan
4944 Chouteau Drive
Kansas City, MO 64119

OZARKS
Ed Heiss
2531 Cherokee
Springfield, MO 65840

ST. LOUIS
Dr. Albert L. Howe
31 York Drive
St. Louis, MO 63144

NEBRASKA

CORNHUSKER
Heber Waldron
525 South 48th Street
Lincoln, NE 68510

NEVADA

SOUTHERN NEVADA
Art Rader
1486 Elizabeth
Las Vegas, NV 89109

NEW JERSEY

NORTH JERSEY
Albert L. Creamer
46 Glen Avenue
Millburn, NJ 07041

TRI-STATE
Frank Reilly
16 Sanford Street
Dover, NJ 07801

WEST JERSEY
George C. Springer
7 McArthur Drive 408 North
Westmont, NJ 08108

NEW YORK

BUFFALO
Harold J. Ahlstrom
158 Stockbridge Avenue
Buffalo, NY 14215

CENTRAL NEW YORK
Frank M. Klock, Jr.
2085 Milton Avenue
Solvay, NY 13209

LONG ISLAND
E. M. Koehler, Jr.
232 Fair Oaks Place
Cedarhurst, NY 11516

MOHAWK & HUDSON
Robert Manwiller
350 Manning Boulevard
Albany, NY 12206

NEW YORK
Herbert G. Frank, Jr.
655 East 14th Street
New York, NY 10009

NORTHERN NEW YORK
C. A. Butterfield
823 Academy Street
Watertown, NY 13601

ONTARIO & WESTERN
John H. Chryn
18 Orchard Street
Middletown, NY 10940

ROCHESTER
Henry J. Pape
104 Estall Road
Rochester, NY 14616

NORTH CAROLINA

EAST CAROLINA
Capt. H. C. Bridgers, Jr.
Box 429
Tarboro, NC 27886

PIEDMONT CAROLINAS
L. G. Robinson
165 Park Fairfax Drive
Charlotte, NC 28208

WARREN COUNTY
Alban C. Fair
P.O. Box 613
Warrenton, NC 27589

WINSTON-SALEM
William Russell
652 Sunset Drive S.W.
Winston-Salem, NC 27103

NORTH DAKOTA

RED RIVER VALLEY
Karl Schiebold
1726-7th Street South
Fargo, ND 58102

OHIO

CINCINNATI
Dan Finfrock
5198 Dee Alva Drive
Fairfield, OH 45014

CONNEAUT
Paul W. Prescott
139 McKinley Drive
Conneaut, OH 44030

MAHONING VALLEY
R. Donald Elser
11025 Sharrott Road
North Lima, OH 44452

MIDWEST
Frederic M. Klein
23724 Lorain Road
North Olmsted, OH 44070

OKLAHOMA

CENTRAL OKLAHOMA
Howard B. Thornton
2936 Bella Vista
Midwest City, OK 73110

NORTHERN OKLAHOMA
Andrew J. Moore
1003 Oklahoma Street
Woodward, OK 73801

OREGON

PACIFIC NORTHWEST
Roger W. Sackett
11550 S.W. Cardinal Terrace
Beaverton, OR 97005

PENNSYLVANIA

BUCKTAIL
Michael H. Bauer, Jr.
228 Church Street
St. Mary's, PA 15857

LACK & WYO VALLEY
William Haussler
1526 East Street
Honesdale, PA 18431

PITTSBURGH
Jerold T. Moyers
156 West Patty Lane
Monroeville, PA 15146

CENTRAL PENNSYLVANIA
Charles W. Winslow
R.D. 2
Lewisburg, PA 17837

LAKE SHORE
James Caldwell
5808 Georgetown Drive
Erie, PA 16509

POTTSTOWN
Henry Keough
274 Prospect Street
Pottstown, PA 19464

CUMBERLAND VALLEY
John C. Marshall
132 North 6th Street
Chambersburg, PA 17201

LANCASTER
Howard S. Fox, Jr.
104 East Poplar Street
Lebanon, PA 17042

SUSQUEHANNA VALLEY
Albert J. Derr
831 Lombardy Drive
Lansdale, PA 19446

HARRISBURG
Howard M. Etter
P.O. Box 57
Shippensburg, PA 17257

LEHIGH VALLEY
Elwood McEllroy
842 St. John Street
Allentown, PA 18102

YORK
Harold E. Grove
45 North Broad Street
York, PA 17403

HAWK MOUNTAIN
Richard J. Diehm
726 Thorn Street
Reading, PA 19601

NEW HOPE
Thomas C. Lightfoot
1061 Beverly Road
Jenkintown, PA 19046

HORSESHOE CURVE
Roy C. Hunt
7 West 4th Avenue
Everett, PA 15537

PHILADELPHIA
Albert J. Pfeiffer, Jr.
220 Lorna Drive
Hatboro, PA 19040

SOUTH CAROLINA

CHARLESTON
Lloyd Willcox
2 King Street
Charleston, SC 29401

TENNESSEE

EAST TENNESSEE
D. W. DeVault
1426 Crescent Drive
Kingsport, TN 37664

NASHVILLE
Robert W. Thurman, Jr.
401 Eatherly Drive
Nashville, TN 37220

OLD SMOKY
Robert D. Henderson
1805 McAlice Drive N.E.
Knoxville, TN 37918

MEMPHIS
Dr. Raymond F. Mayer
400 Goodland Circle
Memphis, TN 38111

NORTH ALABAMA
Jack Daniel
5545 Timmons
Memphis, TN 38117

TENNESSEE VALLEY
Herman H. Lamb
7 Fairhills Drive
Chattanooga, TN 37405

TEXAS

GULF COAST
James R. Gough
3025 Glen Haven Boulevard
Houston, TX 77025

SAN ANTONIO
Cecil K. Beck
2626 McCullough Avenue
San Antonio, TX 78212

UTAH

PROMONTORY
Raymond F. Phelps
2230 Texas Street
Salt Lake City, UT 84109

VERMONT

CHAMPLAIN VALLEY
John L. Gardner
294 Swift Street
South Burlington, VT 05401

VIRGINIA

BLUE RIDGE
Richard T. Myers
3600 Sherwood Place
Lynchburg, VA 24503

OLD DOMINION
Carlton N. McKenney
7731 Brookside Road
Richmond, VA 23229

RIVANNA
Archie Tomlin
Route 1, Box 267
Charlottesville, VA 22901

ROANOKE
Carl S. Jensen
408 Hedgelawn Avenue N.W.
Roanoke, VA 24019

TIDEWATER
R. B. Boushell, Jr.
4008 Greenway Court West
Portsmouth, VA 23702

WASHINGTON
Harry H. Olmsted
1025 Oakcrest Road
Arlington, VA 22202

WINCHESTER
Russell L. Bell
218 West Whitlock Avenue
Winchester, VA 22601

WASHINGTON

INLAND EMPIRE
Lee Tillotson
2627 Southeast Boulevard
Spokane, WA 99203

TACOMA
Melvin L. Prather
7358-28th Avenue S.W.
Seattle, WA 98126

WEST VIRGINIA

COLLIS P. HUNTINGTON
John P. Killoran
407 Circle Drive
Hurricane, WV 25526

WISCONSIN

WISCONSIN
George Drury
2535 North Prospect, #312
Milwaukee, WI 53211

QUEBEC (CANADA)

LAURENTIDE
F. A. Kemp
5950 Molson Street
Montreal, Que., Canada H1Y-3B9

Bibliography
and Suggested Reading

Abdill, George B. *A Locomotive Engineer's Album.* Seattle: Superior Publishing Co., 1965.

————. *Rails West.* Seattle: Superior Publishing Co., 1960.

————. *Pacific Slope Railroads.* Seattle: Superior Publishing Co., 1959.

————. *This Was Railroading.* Seattle: Superior Publishing Co., 1958.

Alexander, Edwin P. *On the Main Line.* New York: Clarkson N. Potter, Bramhall House, 1971.

————. *Down at the Depot.* New York: Clarkson N. Potter, Bramhall House, 1970.

————. *The Pennsylvania Railroad.* New York: Crown Publishers, Bonanza Books, 1967.

————. *The Collector's Book of the Locomotive.* New York: Clarkson N. Potter, Bramhall House, 1966.

————. *Iron Horses: American Locomotives.* New York: Crown Publishers, Bonanza Books, 1941.

Beebe, Lucius. *The Central Pacific & the Southern Pacific Railroads.* Berkeley: Howell-North Press, 1963.

————. *Mr. Pullman's Elegant Palace Car.* Garden City: Doubleday & Co., 1961.

————. *Mansions on Rails.* Berkeley: Howell-North Press, 1959.

————. *Mixed Train Daily.* New York: E. P. Dutton & Co., 1947.

————. *Highball: A Pageant of Trains.* New York: Crown Publishers, Bonanza Books, 1945.

————. *High Iron: A Book of Trains.* New York: Crown Publishers, Bonanza Books, 1938.

Beebe, Lucius and Clegg, Charles. *The Trains We Rode.* Vol. 1. Berkeley: Howell-North Books, 1965

————. *The Trains We Rode.* Vol. 2. Berkeley: Howell-North Books, 1966.

————. *Narrow Gauge in the Rockies.* Berkeley: Howell-North Books, 1958.

————. *Steamcars to the Comstock.* Berkeley: Howell-North Books, 1957.

————. *Hear the Train Blow.* New York: Grossett & Dunlap, 1952.

Bowman, Hank Wieand. *Pioneer Railroads.* Greenwich: Fawcett Books, 1954.

Collias, Joe G. *The Last of Steam.* Berkeley: Howell-North Books, 1960.

Combs, Barry B. *Westward to Promontory.* New York: Garland Books, 1969.

Dorin, Patrick C. *The Domeliners.* Seattle: Superior Publishing Co., 1973.

Dubin, Arthur D. *More Classical Trains.* Milwaukee: Kalmbach Publishing Co., 1974.

————. *Some Classic Trains.* Milwaukee: Kalmbach Publishing Co., 1964.

Ellis, C. Hamilton. *The Lore of the Train.* New York: Crown Publishers, Crescent Books, 1973.

Farrington, Jr., S. Kip. *Railroads of Today.* New York: Coward-McCann, 1949.

————. *Railroading from the Rear End.* New York: Coward-McCann, 1946.

————. *Railroading from the Head End.* Garden City: Doubleday, Doran & Co., 1943.

Harlow, Alvin F. *Old Waybills.* New York: D. Appleton-Century Co., 1934.

Henry, Robert Selph. *Trains.* Indianapolis: Bobbs-Merrill Co., 1934.

Hertz, Louis H. *Collecting Model Trains.* New York: Simmons-Boardman Publishing Corp., 1956.

Holbrook, Stewart H. *The Story of American Railroads.* New York: Crown Publishers, 1947.

Hornug, Clarence P. *Wheels across America.* New York: A. S. Barnes & Co., 1959.

Howard, Robert West. *The Great Iron Trail.* New York: Crown Publishers, Bonanza Books, 1962.

Hubbard, Freeman H. *Great Trains of All Times.* New York: Grossett & Dunlap, 1962.

_____. *Railroad Avenue.* New York: McGraw-Hill Book Co., Whittlesey House, 1945.

Hungerford, Edward. *The Story of the Baltimore & Ohio Railroad.* 2 vols. New York: G. P. Putnam's Sons, 1928.

Kinert, Reed. *Early American Steam Locomotives.* New York: Crown Publishers, Bonanza Books, 1962.

Kraus, George. *High Road to Promontory.* Palo Alto: American West Publishing Co., 1969.

Laut, Agnes C. *The Romance of the Rails.* 2 vols. New York: Robert M. McBride & Co., 1929.

O'Connell, John. *Railroad Album.* Chicago: Popular Mechanics Press, 1954.

Phillips, Lance. *Yonder Comes the Train.* New York: A. S. Barnes & Co., 1965.

Reed, Robert C. *Train Wrecks.* New York: Crown Publishers, Bonanza Books, 1968.

Reynolds, Roger. *Famous American Trains.* New York: Grossett & Dunlap, 1934.

Shaw, Frederic. *Casey Jones' Locker.* San Francisco: Hesperian House Book Publishers, 1959.

Westing, Fred. *The Locomotives That Baldwin Built.* Seattle: Superior Publishing Co., 1966.

Wheaton, J. Lane. *Commodore Vanderbilt.* New York: Alfred A. Knopf, 1942.

Woods, Charles R. *The North Pacific.* Seattle: Superior Publishing Co., 1968.

_____. *Lines West.* Seattle: Superior Publishing Co., 1967.

Ziel, Ron. *The Twilight of the Steam Locomotive.* New York: Grossett & Dunlap, 1963.

CURRENT RAILROAD PERIODICALS

The Great World of Model Railroading

Model Railroad Craftsman

Model Railroader

Passenger Train Journal

Rail Classics

Rail Fan

Railroad Magazine

Railroad Modeler

Trains

The Railroadiana Collectors Association, Inc., was formed in November, 1971, and incorporated on November 19, 1971, as a nonprofit corporation wholly owned by the members. The purpose of the RCAI is to promote interest in railroadiana collecting and railroad history by establishing contact between people of similiar interests through the publication of the quarterly *Railroadiana Express* and the annual *Directory.* The *Express* carries articles of interest about railroadiana, railroad history, lists new members with their interests, and offers classified ads to the members. Write to Dan Moss, Secretary, 405 Byron Avenue, Mobile, AL 36609.

Trains magazine, a monthly periodical, carries a column entitled "Running Extra," which lists various museums and railroad clubs across the country and also current rail fan excursion trips. The column is a good source for making contacts and obtaining additional information.

A bibliography of railroad literature may be obtained free on request from the Association of American Railroads, Washington, D.C. Another helpful organization is the Railway & Locomotive Historical Society, Baker Library, Harvard University, Cambridge, MA.

Index